He Speaks to Me

PREPARING TO HEAR FROM GOD

Priscilla Shirer

LifeWay Press®
Nashville, Tennessee

Published by LifeWay Press®
© 2005 • Priscilla Shirer
Eighth printing 2011

ISBN 978-1-4158-2093-3
Item 001269686

Dewey Decimal Classification Number: 248.843
Subject Headings: SPIRITUAL LIFE \ WOMEN—RELIGIOUS LIFE \ GOD—WILL

Unless otherwise noted, all Scripture quotations are taken from the Holman Christian Standard
Bible®, ©Copyright 2001 Holman Bible Publishers, Nashville, TN. Used by permission.
Scripture quotations identified NRSV are from the New Revised Standard Version of the Bible,
copyright © 1989 by the Division of Christian Education of the National Council
of Churches of Christ in the United States of America. Used by permission.
Scripture quotations identified The Message are from The Message. Copyright © 1993, 1994,
1995, 1996, 2000, 2001, 2002. Used by permission of NavPress Publishing Group.
Scripture quotations identified NASB are from the New American Standard Bible,
Copyright © 1960, 1962, 1963, 1968, 1971, 1972, 1973, 1975, 1977, 1995
by the Lockman Foundation. Used by permission. (*www.lockman.org*).
Scripture quotations identified NLT are from the Holy Bible,
New Living Translation, copyright © 1996.
Scripture quotations identified ASV are from the American Standard Version.

The source for the Greek and Hebrew definitions used throughout the study
have been taken from *Strong's Exhaustive Concordance of the Bible*,
published by Holman Bible Publishers, Nashville, Tennessee.

To order additional copies of this resource, write to LifeWay Church Resources Customer
Service; One LifeWay Plaza; Nashville, TN 37234-0013; fax (615) 251-5933;
phone (800) 458-2772; order online at *www.lifeway.com;* e-mail
orderentry@lifeway.com; or visit the LifeWay Christian Store serving you.

Printed in the United States of America.

Leadership and Adult Publishing
LifeWay Church Resources
One LifeWay Plaza
Nashville, TN 37234-0175

Contents

Foreword. 5

Introduction 6

Viewer Guide: Session 1 7
Week 1: A Simple Relationship 8

Viewer Guide: Session 2 27
Week 2: A Single-Minded Worship 28

Viewer Guide: Session 3 45
Week 3: A Set-Apart Holiness 46

Viewer Guide: Session 4 65
Week 4: A Still Attentiveness. 66

Viewer Guide: Session 5 83
Week 5: A Sold-Out Hunger 84

Viewer Guide: Session 6 103
Week 6: A Servant Spirit 104

Leader Guide. 122

Christian Growth Study Plan. 128

About the Author

PRISCILLA SHIRER is a Bible teacher and motivational speaker. She is a graduate of the University of Houston, with a Bachelor's degree in Communications, and Dallas Theological Seminary, with a Master's degree in Biblical Studies. For over 10 years she has been a conference speaker for major corporations, organizations, and Christian audiences across the United States and the world.

Priscilla is now in full-time ministry to women. Her ministry is focused on the expository teaching of the Word of God. She desires to see women not only know the uncompromising truths of Scripture intellectually but experience them practically by the power of the Holy Spirit.

Priscilla is the author of *A Jewel in His Crown, A Jewel in His Crown Journal,* and *And We Are Changed: Transforming Encounters with God.* She is the daughter of pastor, speaker, and well-known author Dr. Tony Evans. She is married to her best friend, Jerry. The couple reside in Dallas, Texas with their two sons Jackson and Jerry Jr.

About the Study

AS YOU BEGIN YOUR STUDY, keep several things in mind. The material in this book is divided into five days of individual study and one small-group session each week where you will process with others what you have studied. The small-group sessions provide an excellent opportunity to share what the Lord is teaching you as well as learn from what the Lord is teaching other women in your group. Each day of individual study will take about 30 minutes. The personal learning activities are designed to help you apply to your life what you are learning. Please don't skip over these activities. The activities also will prepare you for your small-group session where you will be asked to share some of your responses.

Consider the following suggestions to make your study more meaningful.

- Trust the Holy Spirit to be your teacher. Ask Him for guidance as you seek to better prepare yourself to hear from the Lord.
- Keep a spiritual journal of God's activity in your life as well as your response to Him throughout the study. When God speaks, it is important to record it. Your memory will not always recall these "special moments," but your journal will!
- Live out your growing relationship with and knowledge of God. Be willing to step out of your comfort zone and share freely with others what the Lord is teaching you.

May God bless you as you seek to listen and respond to God's voice.

Foreword

As I stared at the title to this Bible study, I felt the emotion well in my throat. At the risk of sounding dramatic, I can't think of a spiritual reality that moves and astonishes me more on a daily basis than God's willingness to speak to us and give us ears to hear. I never get over feeling completely amazed any time something confirms that I really did hear God on a matter. To me, the whole process is miraculous. The first recorded words out of the mouth of God erupted a universe out of absolute nothingness. His words alter anything that truly hears them. You and I want to hear them. Discern them. Respond to them.

Communication is the essence of all relationships. Like most married couples, my husband, Keith, and I have very different personalities and ways of expressing ourselves. We've had to learn how to read one another and speak one another's "language." I remember days when my daughters would try to tell me something from one end of the house while I was in the other. So much lay between us—walls, radios, a blaring TV—that I could faintly hear their voices but I couldn't understand what they were saying. "Come closer so I can hear you better!" Without the ability to speak, hear, and respond, we'd never have experienced true family. The only thing interacting would have been our dirty clothes in the washer.

I'd heard of Priscilla Shirer for a year or two before I finally got to meet her face-to-face. I knew I was going to be impressed with her because I'd heard such wonderful things from people whose "taste" I trusted. Still, I was totally floored. Not only was she beautiful, articulate, and smart, she was warm and extremely likeable. I might have been jealous of Priscilla—she's so darling, wise, and young, after all—but her way was so disarming I couldn't be anything but drawn to her. If you don't know her already, may I have the honor of introducing you to my little sister in Christ and my soul-sister in the study of God's Word? Please meet Priscilla Shirer. Study with her, learn from her, and fall in love with her. This study won't be her last but, for starters, what topic could be more critical than learning to position ourselves to hear the voice of God and respond to it?

I can't wait to see what God's going to do with Priscilla. I'll be cheering her on all the way …while choking on the dust.

Go, girl. I'm nuts about you.

Beth Moore

Introduction

WHY SHOULD BELIEVERS BE SATISFIED with "hand-me-down" revelation? Why do we settle for the Word of the Lord revealed to someone else and passed on to us as if God does not speak to us individually? This shouldn't satisfy us. He desires to speak to us personally. He wants us to hear His voice, understand, and obey. Many have become satisfied with a mediocre Christian existence that sits on the sidelines while those we consider more spiritual have a relationship with God.

One of the rights and privileges we have as followers is that our Lord speaks to us one-on-one. He meets us *where* we are despite *who* we are and reveals His will for our lives. I want to encourage you to dig deep into the presence of God and listen for the voice of God as He speaks to us all.

I see something interesting in many biblical examples. Before God spoke He often waited until they had shown interest in receiving His word. For example, the resurrected Jesus gently called Mary's name only after she came to the tomb desperately seeking the body of her Savior (John 20). He spoke to a woman with a medical problem only after she forced her way through a crowd and touched the hem of His cloak (Luke 8). David got clear direction from God regarding several major decisions only after "he inquired of the Lord" (1 Sam. 23, 30). A 12-year-old boy named Samuel heard the voice of God calling him but only after he positioned himself directly outside the holy of holies (1 Sam. 3).

Could our inability to hear God have less to do with His desire to speak and more to do with our lack of preparedness to hear? The Lord speaks clearly but those most likely to hear are those who have correctly positioned themselves.

On many occasions the Lord has gently reminded me that "it is [my] sin that causes the separation between me and God" (Isa. 59:2). I am the one standing in the way of receiving His fresh, personal, and revealing Word. While we are waiting on God to do His part, He could be waiting on us to do ours!

This study focuses on what we need to do to prepare ourselves to hear God when He chooses to speak. We will look at a familiar story that captured my attention. In 1 Samuel 3, we find a young man who grew up surrounded by religious activity. I can relate to that. Yet the difference between Samuel and me is that He heard God's voice. For much of my Christian life, I didn't! I began a journey to discover the characteristics God must have seen in Samuel that made Him desire to speak and made Samuel capable of hearing. Those six characteristics will unfold over the next six weeks.

I believe God is going to reveal Himself and His plan for you in new ways. Make a commitment to be obedient to whatever He says. If you do, I promise you will not be disappointed in the glorious results!

God bless you as we study God's Word and listen for His voice together,

Priscilla Shirer

Viewer Guide
Session 1

Now the boy Samuel was ministering to the LORD before Eli. And word from the Lord was rare in those days, visions were infrequent.
—1 Samuel 3:1

Samuel was a ___child___ *3 yrs old (weaned) brought to Eli - dedicated*
2:18 Samuel ministering before Lord

Samuel did not yet know the LORD, nor had the word of the LORD yet been revealed to him.
—1 Samuel 3:7

"Permit the children to come to Me, and do not hinder them, for the kingdom of God belongs to such as these."
—Luke 18:16

2:26 Sam cont. to grow in stature + in favor c the Lord + men

1. Jesus welcomes _____.

2. Jesus makes a _____ to children.

The manifestation of the power, presence, and voice of God is available to you now!

A Simple Relationship

SOME OF THE MOST AMAZING LESSONS I have learned have come from children. The 10 year old poverty stricken Haitian girl who smiled at me during a mission trip taught me we can be content in the midst of horrible circumstances. My curious nephew who touches everything in my house reminds me that childlike curiosity stimulates continued growth. And the love I feel for my sons has been the Lord's tool to show me how much He loved me to give up His Son for my sin.

Children teach us the deep things of God. Christ himself saw an invaluable tool in children because He used them to teach His followers.

The very first characteristic we learn about Samuel was that He was just a child when he heard God speak. In a nation of adults God was looking for the simplicity of a child. At 12 years old, Samuel heard God speak.

DAY 1
A Simple Obedience

DAILY BREAD

He called a child to Him. Matthew 18:2

After Jackson's quiet time yesterday, books and toys were scattered everywhere. I asked him to clean up his play area. Excited to move on with the rest of his day, he bounded to his feet and quickly put everything in its proper place.

When he finished, I smiled, opened my arms to him, and said, "Come here sweetie." But Jackson didn't want to come to me. In fact, my instruction seemed to repel him. He ran from me!

I marveled that he had easily made the effort to clean up his play area, but he fought against the simple obedience required to come to me. Then I thought, *how like our relationship to God.* We often run from God's request for our attention. We struggle against God's desire that we simply spend time with Him. Why is it sometimes difficult for us to follow the simple instructions the Lord gives us?

The Basics of Obedience

The disciples lived with Jesus. They saw Jesus heal and heard Him preach. They watched Him feed five thousand people with only five barley loaves and two fish. They even saw Him walk on water. Yet when Jesus wanted to teach them about obedience, He didn't dazzle them with miracles. He pointed to the basics of childhood.

In Matthew 18 Jesus used a child's willingness to obey to illustrate the beauty of simple obedience. For three years Jesus had been teaching and preaching. Thousands had heard His messages and seen His miracles. So why did the great teacher and miracle worker use a little one to show adults what true obedience looks like? Jesus called and the child came.

What does Matthew 11:20 tell us about how some adults responded to Jesus' teaching and miracles?

did not repent — proud

Which of the following best describes how you normally respond to Christ's Word?
- ❏ rebel
- ❏ argue with God
- ❏ question
- ❏ run away
- ❏ immediately obey
- ❏ other *slowly; ponder - is it ? doubt was it his voice ?*

Children have several traits that create the openness and willingness the Lord wants adults to recapture. They are naturally curious, using their curiosity to learn. They are excited by learning something new and delight in discovering new truths. That childish excitement is magical. It points to pure faith and total trust. My sister, the Lord wants us to regain these traits from childhood. I want a child's willing response to Jesus to impact my own relationship with Him.

What steps of simple obedience is the Lord requiring of you? (I've included examples from my list in the margin.)

better care of this temple (eat/exercise)

boldly speak

finances

- serve my family graciously, willingly, and as a priority
- regularly spend time with God
- control eating habits
- honor my spouse's authority

Let's commit to obeying the Lord when we hear His voice. We must repent for the times we have ignored, fought against, or criticized His instructions.

The Sacrifice of Obedience

Unfortunately, balking against the Lord's instructions often seems easier than following them because obedience requires sacrifice. While our personal sacrifices may differ, they will always be required of us.

Look back at the list I shared with you of simple ways the Lord has asked me to obey Him. To fulfill those, I must make some sacrifices.

- To serve my family, I must often forfeit my own desires.
- To spend time with Him regularly, I must say "no" to other activities.
- To control my eating, I must not overindulge.
- To control my spending habits, I must not buy every outfit that turns my head.
- To honor my husband's authority, I must release the desire to be in control.

Sacrifices often feel like I am giving up something valuable. I have to remind myself that joy and and freedom always lie in obedience. Each of the sacrifices in my list ultimately results in my good. Each of the issues I surrender really contain poison that, if kept, will kill the wonderful future God has for me. Author Eugene Peterson expressed the idea wonderfully: "You know well enough from your own experience that there are some acts of so-called freedom that destroy freedom. Offer yourselves to sin, for instance, and it's your last free act. But offer yourselves to the ways of God and the freedom never quits" (Rom. 6:1, *The Message*).

What sacrifices are you currently making in obedience to the Lord?

relationship ships - honor marriage

serving mom / dad

Look closely at the following passages. What sacrifices did these individuals make by walking obediently with God?

Peter and the apostles (Acts 5:17-29,40)
(flogged)
arrested. persecuted - set free from jail

Daniel, Shadrach, Meshach, and Abednego (Dan. 3:14-19)
thrown into Blazing fire

Abraham (Gen. 22:1-3)
Sacrifice his son

(Potphar's wife)

Joseph (Gen. 39:10-20) *false testimony — put in prison*

Hosea (Hos. 1:2-3; 3:1-3) *take adulterous wife + children reconciliation ē adulterous wife*

The Reward of Obedience

Obedience will not always be easy, but it will always be worth it. Obedience to God always brings reward.

Describe how the characters in the previous activity were rewarded.

Peter (Acts 5:40-42) *felt honored thru persecution never stopped teaching + proclaiming good news*

Daniel and his friends (Dan. 3:27) *fire did not harm them*

Abraham (Gen. 22:16-18) *Blessed - all nations on earth Blessed - given cities of enemies*

Joseph (Gen. 39:21; 41:41-42) *Lord ē Him (Joseph) in prison - favored - put in charge of prison and eventually and Pharaoh in charge of whole land*

Hosea (Hos. 3) *Return of Israelites to the Lord*

Carefully read Deuteronomy 28:1-14. List the rewards promised to those who obey the Lord.

Bless wherever go; childbirth, crops. livestock defeat enemies, prosper, become Holy people rain for crops - always be on top.

TAKE ACTION

By following the Lord in <u>obedience</u>, we are <u>preparing</u> or positioning ourselves t<u>o hear</u> <u>His voice</u>. By sacrificing our own desires for His, we are aligning ourselves with His will and opening the door to receive His blessings. Remember the example of the little boy in Matthew 18? The disciples had a more intimate relationship with Jesus than the child did, yet Jesus chose the child to illustrate simple obedience. This shows us that intimacy with God doesn't always translate to practical obedience

In what areas do you feel your relationship with God is lacking in practical obedience?

finances

Write a prayer asking God to help you become more obedient to Him in these areas.

Forgive me for spending more than comes in - Help me to be a better steward of H.

DAY 2
A Simple Beginning

You've chosen this Bible study because you want to prepare yourself to hear God's voice and receive wisdom from Him. Proverbs 1:7 and 9:10 respond to that need with the same basic message: "The fear of the Lord is the beginning of wisdom." In fact, the phrase "The fear of the Lord" is so important to the quest for spiritual wisdom that Solomon repeated it 11 times in Proverbs.

Proverbs 1:7 says, "The fear of the Lord is the beginning of knowledge." In Hebrew, "<u>the fear</u>" is *Yir' ah* meaning "to <u>reverence or respect</u>." "Beginning" translates to *re' shiyth* which means "the essence." And "knowledge," *da'ath* in Hebrew, means "perception, discernment, spiritual understanding."

Based on these definitions, rewrite the phrase "the fear of the Lord is the beginning of knowledge" in your own words in the margin.

Reverence & respect for God is the very essence of spiritual understanding

Spiritual perception and discernment come from reverencing and honoring God. I paraphrased the verse: "Respect for the Lord is the essence of spiritual understanding." To hear God's voice we absolutely must be willing to recognize and appropriately respond to Him. Showing God respect opens our hearts and our spiritual ears to clearly hear from Him.

Now let's look at the variations in usage applied to Proverbs 9:10. Here the word *beginning* is taken from the Hebrew word *ta'chilliah* which means "the prerequisite, starting point." *Wisdom* in this passage comes from the Hebrew term *chokmah* which means "skillful, wisdom, wisely."

Using these definitions, rewrite the phrase "the fear of the Lord is the beginning of wisdom."

The starting point (or prerequisite) to to wisely respect God

In our quest to hear God's voice, we cannot gain spiritual insight or wisdom if we begin at the wrong place. Our desire to hear from Him must begin with reverence. Respecting God is not only the essence of wisdom, it is also the prerequisite for it.

Spiritual Wisdom

Notice the progression: Proverbs 1:7 promises spiritual understanding as a result of respecting God while Proverbs 9:10 goes a step further by saying that we will also acquire wisdom. Spiritual wisdom combines knowledge with skill and applies it to practical situations. Fearing God, for instance, not only opens the door to spiritual insight (knowledge); it goes a step further and allows us to usefully and skillfully apply that insight so it practically transforms our lives. After all, what good is knowledge if we don't know how to apply it?

- What good is a brain surgeon who made straight A's in medical school but has never applied his knowledge in surgery?
- Who cares about the high academic scores of an airline captain who has never actually flown a commercial plane?
- What's the importance of the many framed degrees on the wall in your OB/GYN's office if your child is the first she's ever delivered?

I don't know about you, but tested skill matters much more to me than knowledge.

Fearing God does not mean that we should feel terror. It points to reverence and respect. *The Holman Bible Dictionary* refers to this as religious fear and defines it as "the human response to the presence of God." This type of fear combines reverence for God's majesty and respect of His power. It is a "reverential regard and awe that comes out of recognition and submission to the divine." Our ability to obtain wisdom from God begins and grows with our ability and willingness to fear Him.

DAILY BREAD
"Truly I tell you, unless you change and become like children, you will never enter the kingdom of heaven."
Matthew 18:3, NRSV

13

Write your own paraphrase of Ecclesiastes 12:13 below.

love, respect & reverence of God -will (help keep his commandments) bring our obedience

I love *The Message* translation of this verse: "The last and final word is this: Fear God. Do what He tells you." A healthy fear of God precedes obedience to God.

Practical Respect

When you and I respect someone, our actions automatically reflect it. As a child, when I was disobedient, I remember my parents saying, "You don't respect me the way you should because if you did you would obey me." When we see God and respect Him for Who He is, an attitude of submission and obedience should stem from our desire to honor Him. The way we relate to the Lord demonstrates the respect we have for Him.

What does your current level of practical obedience reveal about your respect for God?

I don't respect Him.   I give conditional respect.   I give total respect.

Often we wait for God to speak to us, but have we done our part in preparing to hear from Him? Are we reverencing, respecting, and obeying Him? Without the proper preparation, we cannot gain the knowledge and wisdom He provides.

prepared to hear from Him - our part

Honoring God is key to hearing from God.

Romans 1:21-22 explains what happens when people who have only a head knowledge of God refuse to honor Him. Fill in the blanks.

"Their thinking became _____ *futile* _____ and their senseless minds were _____ *darkened* _____. *foolish*

Claiming to be _____ *wise* _____, they became _____ *fools* _____."

Intellectual knowledge can help us know about God, but only a personal relationship with Him will lead us to a saving knowledge. That intimate, personal relationship leads us to respect, honor, and reverence God. This is where true wisdom begins.

TAKE ACTION

List some specific areas in which you desire to more closely obey the Lord.

_____

_____

Honoring God is key to hearing from God. Our ability to hear His voice begins when we reverence Him through simple obedience. Knowing God is not enough; we must fear and obey Him.

Let's ask the Lord to forgive us for any rebellion against His instructions. Let's commit to earnestly reverencing Him through our actions.

Close today's lesson by picking one thing from the list you made above that you can begin to work on today. Write that item below and list the steps you can take today to walk in obedience in that area.

change auto withdrawl B of M. card — stop using it

Call tomorrow

DAY 3
A Simple Humility

When I was a year old, my parents began a 10-member church that has now ballooned to include over 7,000 members. As the preacher's kid, I automatically became the center of attention. Church members treated me as their little girl, and I grew used to everyone catering to and taking care of me. The members meant well, but their good intentions created problems for me as I became an adult.

I constantly have to work on humility, consciously striving to consider others before myself. But I know I am not alone in my struggle to remain humble. Consider the conflict that arose among the disciples.

DAILY BREAD

"Whoever humbles himself like this child—this one is the greatest in the kingdom of heaven."

Matthew 18:4

What had the disciples been arguing about according to Matthew 18:1?

who is greatest in Kingdom of God (Heaven)

In what areas of your life do you face similar conflict?

❑ marriage ❑ work ❑ family ❑ neighborhood
❑ school ❑ church ❑ other: _____

On the heels of this argument Jesus tells the disciples to humble themselves like a child. _trusting, unpretentious_

What Is Humility?

The Bible Exposition Commentary says that true humility means knowing, accepting, and being yourself—your best self—for God's glory.[1] It means avoiding two extremes: thinking less of yourself than you ought to (as did Moses when God called him; see Ex. 3:11), or thinking more of yourself than you ought to (see Rom. 12:3). A truly humble person does not deny the gifts God has given her, nor brag about them as if they are by her own doing.

Humility is the ability to think of others, putting their needs before your own. My Aunt Elizabeth is one of the most humble people I know. Serving faithfully and quietly in our church for over 25 years, she is constantly more concerned with the feelings of others than with her own. In fact, she always works with a smile and a positive attitude. Though she rarely receives applause or public recognition for the wonderful job she does with the children at our church, her car is often the first in the parking lot and the last to leave after service on Sunday mornings. Her humility and dedication are such an inspiration to me.

Pride the opposite of humility

List three individuals you know who demonstrate humility. Briefly describe how humility is evidenced by their actions.

1. _John Loney - silent, confident, knowledge_

2. _Jeanne Northfield - quiet, strong, gifted serves_

3. _Cheri C. - gives credit to God_

What Is Humility Not?

Pride—the antithesis of humility—is the compost heap on which myriad other problems and sins grow. Pride causes us to think we can do more than we can and convinces us we deserve special treatment, recognition, or honor. Pride causes us to think less of others and too much of ourselves.

Read Matthew 18:1-2 again.

Comparing the disciples' approach to Jesus versus the child's approach shows a practical truth about humility. Pride leads us to force our way into a situation while humility waits. *To humble gives grace*

According to 1 Peter 5:5, what is God's response to pride?

opposes the proud – arrogant self serving

The Result of Pride

In Luke 9:46-48, we gain another insight into the situation presented in Matthew 18. Verse 46 reveals that the discussion over greatness caused an argument among this band of brothers. The disciples were actually arguing over which of them was the greatest. What created the argument? Pride. Relational problems with friends or family often indicate that pride is on the rise. We need to ask to what degree our pride gets in the way of reconciliation.

Pray

Are you currently have any strained relationships? ☑ yes ☐ no *skip - proud - more*
If yes, ask the Lord to check the condition of your heart.
Ask Him to reveal to you the part pride plays in your conflict.

List their names below and prayerfully consider how you can walk in practical humility in your relationship with them. Write your thoughts beside each persons name.

judge others – because I understand scripture Godly principles better

Over time, as you implement these changes, come back to this portion of the lesson and list the changes you are seeing in your relationships.

Another indicator pride was present appears in what happened just before the disciples argued over which of them would be greatest in the kingdom.

What revelation did Jesus give to the disciples in Luke 9:44-45?

Son of Man will betrayed into hands of man

How did they respond to His message (vv. 45-46)?

did not understand (or grasp it) → fear - afraid to ask Him

17

The disciples overlooked news of Christ's impending death because they were too concerned with themselves to concentrate on His words. Pride is a distraction. It causes us to bypass important and pertinent issues because we are consumed with ourselves. Often Jesus wants to reveal important information to us, but our prideful hearts get in the way of our ability to hear the message. Humility, on the other hand, clears the pathway for us to hear God.

According to Luke 1:52, what is the difference between how God responds to pride and how He responds to humility?

opposes proud; gives Grace to the humble

God's Response to Humility

God spoke to prophets in visions dreams

Moses was called the most humble man on the face of the earth (see Num. 12:3). He was a leader of integrity who fulfilled the duties of his office despite opposition from members of his own family. He submitted to the authority of God.

How was God's relationship with Moses different than with any other prophet (Num. 12:5-8)?

Spoke ɔ̄ him face to face ɔ̄ clarity. Moses saw form of the Lord

Because of Moses' humility the Lord spoke clearly and personally to him in a way that He did not speak to others.

Read the verses below and list one thing each verse teaches about humility. *(far away from proud)*

Psalm 138:6 *Lord looks on the lowly (humble)*

Who is like the Lord our God, Who is enthroned on high, Who humbles Himself to behold (The things that are) in heaven and in the earth? Psalm 113:5-6, NASB.

Isaiah 57:15 *I (the Lord) live with the contrite & lowly in spirit)*

Isaiah 66:2 *I esteem; the humble & contrite in spirit*

James 4:6 *gives grace to humble   Prov 3:34*

James 4:10 *Lord lifts up the humble*

Jesus is the best physical example we have of true humility (see Phil. 2:5-7). He is the visible manifestation of the Father's character. Psalm 113:5-6 (see margin) reveals that the enthroned God of the universe "humbles Himself." He humbles Himself to behold all His creatures, though He is infinitely above them.

Contrite — crushed broken

TAKE ACTION

What, according to the following verses, should prompt humility in us? *[handwritten: Isaiah realizing who he was in view of the Lord Almighty]*

Isaiah 6:5 *[handwritten: reverent, honor – of the Lord Almighty (being unclean lips)]*

Luke 5:8 *[handwritten: recognize our sinfulness when we see awesomeness of Jesus]*

How can you begin to implement the principle Jesus taught in Luke 14:7-11?

[handwritten: places of honor at table – humble will be exalted.]

<u>Humility</u> should be the <u>natural outpouring of hearts grateful to the Lord</u>. When we consider all the King has done for us, given us, and forgiven us, our hearts should be overjoyed. We should humbly submit to Him like children gratefully submitting to a loving parent.

DAY 4
A Simple Trust

My 17-month-old son trusts me. He often demonstrates that trust by jumping from the top of the stairs into my arms. Of course it scares me to death—especially when I am not paying full attention and he jumps anyway!

As we become adults, trusting can become more difficult. Life experiences lead to a lack of trust. We become more self-sufficient. Yet, Jesus desires that we <u>approach Him with total trust</u> and <u>believe in Him</u> with the simplicity of a child. It takes more than humility to believe in God and respond to Him. It takes trust.

What happens between childhood and adulthood that causes children and adults to respond differently to God?

[handwritten: trust is put toward men who disappoint]

How has your faith in the Lord changed since you first entered into a relationship with Him?

[handwritten: eyes & mind look to Jesus He is trustworthy only]

A Childs Belief → pisteuo - place complete confidence int

Complete Confidence

In Matthew 18:6 Christ uses the Greek word pisteuo to refer to the child's belief. It means "to think to be true, to place complete confidence in." I tried to make a list of things or people I can place complete confidence in but it was pretty short. Only One has earned my complete confidence.

Write Hebrews 11:6 in your own words.

Faith (Belief) is essential to please God we must acknowledge & Believe that he exists

What does the last line of this verse promise those who diligently seek Him?

He rewards those who "diligently" seek him

How does your life confirm that God rewards those who trust Him?

I am Blessed!

The Consequence of Unbelief

Numbers 20:8-12 demonstrates Moses' lack of faith in God's instructions.

What did God specifically instruct Moses to do (v. 8)?

Take staff. speak to the rock

How did Moses disobey (v. 11)?

Struck the rock twice ē staff

What consequences did he have to face as a result (v. 12)?

will Not bring Israelites into the Land

lack of trust, did not Honor me as Holy in the in side in

Notice God's reprimand comes not for simply disobeying but rather for not believing God. Failure to do exactly what God asks, regardless of how strange or incomplete His instructions seem, shows lack of faith in God Himself. It shows we don't trust that He is God and knows what's best. By not doing what He tells us, we are saying that we don't think God is wise enough or capable enough to handle our situations.

Recall a time you received instructions from God that seemed strange and you didn't want to follow. What happened as a result of your action or inaction?

Lack of obedience = lack of trust that He Knows best

feel distant - empty; far away from God communication interrupted

There are times in my marriage when I want to say something specific to my husband, but the Lord clearly instructs me not to speak at all. And I admit that sometimes when His instructions seem strange, I rebel against them. Every time, I wish I hadn't. My words only escalate arguments and cause discord in my relationship with my husband. I may "win" an argument with my own actions but at a great cost. God's way is always better, but sometimes I fail to trust Him.

In Numbers 20 Moses did not follow God's instructions. But what miracle happened when he struck the rock (v. 11)?

they got water

What does this reveal about God's grace in times of our disobedience?

Covers the Sin

The people received the water they needed, but Moses and Aaron still suffered the consequences of unbelief. Moses prayed that he and the others would see the land God promised, but his request was not fulfilled because he failed to trust God.

Rewrite Matthew 21:22 in your own words.

If you believe - put your trust in me completely - your prayers will be answered

Could the cause of our unanswered prayers be our lack of childlike pisteuo?

Let's stop and pray, asking the Lord to reveal areas where we operate outside the realm of faith. Ask Him to show you when you are not obeying His instructions, thinking instead that your way is better than His. Let's thank Him for His continued grace, and admit the areas where we lack full trust in His instructions.

The following verses show the importance of faith in our relationship to the Lord. Write key words beside each to remind you of their meanings.

Isaiah 7:9 *stand firm in faith (or won't stand at all)*

John 3:18 *Condemnation for those who do not believe in Jesus*

John 8:24 *dead in sins - if don't believe I am the one who I claim to be.*

Hebrews 3:12 *don't have a unbelieving heart that turns away -*

TAKE ACTION

Your level of action reveals your level of faith. False faith says, "I believe," but then does nothing to prove it. God calls us to act on what we say we believe! If you have the *pisteuo* faith God requires, act on it today. What are you waiting for? He is ready to take you to a new level in Him.

In Cana – son of royal officier sick in Capernaum

Read John 4:46-53, taking careful note of verse 50. What did the royal official do that showed his faith in Jesus?

took Jesus at his word & departed

What actions should you take to show your complete trust in God?

_____

_____

DAY 5
A Simple Dependence

This week we have explored the basics of placing ourselves in a position to hear from God. We've looked at the importance of being obedient, of fearing the Lord and obtaining wisdom, of remaining humble, and of trusting God's plans above our own. Today we'll look at how our dependence on God may affect how He speaks to us.

Small babies depend completely on their parents. Without an adult's assistance and love, they cannot survive. God does not intend for us to remain babies, but He does intend for us to be that dependent on Him. Our society deplores dependency and praises self-sufficiency. Unfortunately, we often rely on ourselves for those things we should lean on Him to provide.

For what achievements, experiences, or blessings have you been tempted to take credit?

_____

In today's Bible verse, Psalm 131:2, David describes dependence on God. He pens these words while considering the high honor of assuming the throne of Israel. This powerful man who will soon be king doesn't credit himself for the blessings in his life (see 1 Sam. 16:1-12; 17:45-50). Instead, he forms a deeper dependence on God, trusting in Him as a child trusts a loving parent.

David begins his conversation with God not by focusing on his accomplishments and greatness but by confessing his inadequacy (see Ps. 131:1). The imagery of a child was already on David's mind, but Jesus had to bring a child to the attention of the disciples in Matthew 18.

The Bible does not tell us the words the disciples used in their argument over personal greatness, but the phrases from David's prayer likely differed from those used by the disciples.

> Put yourself in the place of the arguing disciples in Matthew 18:1. Write three statements that contrast David's words from Psalm 131:1. Plan to share your statements with your group. I've given you my example.

DAILY BREAD

I have calmed and quieted myself like a little weaned child with its mother; I am like a little child.
Psalm 131:2

David	Disciples
My heart is not proud.	I sure want to be recognized.
My eyes are not haughty.	*Look at me*
I do not involve myself in great matters.	*I want to be 1st*
I do not involve myself in things too difficult for me.	*I want to be in middle of things*

With which list do your thoughts and conversation most closely align?
❏ David's ❏ the disciples'

David's words demonstrate his inadequacy and complete dependence on the Lord. The disciples thought they were not only adequate but superior.

> Rate your dependence quotient in the following areas: 5 represents the highest level of dependency on God and 1 represents the lowest. Circle your response.

Finances	1	②	3	4	5
Family	1	2	3	4	⑤
Marriage	1	2	3	4	5
Parenting	1	2	3	④	5
Career	1	2	3	④	5

Circle the category in which you've made the greatest progress in trusting God in the past year. Pause to thank God for the areas where you've grown. Ask His assistance in depending on Him in more difficult areas.

As a speaker and Bible teacher, I talk to thousands of women every year. I am so grateful for this exciting and interesting journey. I've learned, however, that I have to be careful not to rely on my communication skills or familiarity with the message. When I rely on familiarity rather than relying on the power of the Holy Spirit, the message lacks power and anointing. On the other hand, when I depend on the Lord and confess my inadequacy, He touches hearts in ways I never could.

Reread Psalm 131:2 on page 24 and check the things David declares he has done.

☑ calmed his soul ☐ made an offering
☐ proclaimed God's name ☑ quieted his soul

David mentions the steps his soul has undergone in reaching dependence on God: calming and quieting. These steps in turn led his soul to rest. Let's look at each of these to discover what we must do to become dependent on God.

The Calmed Soul

First David says, "I have calmed ... myself." Calming is an action of which David has to take control. He compares the effort of calming his soul with the activity of weaning a baby from its mother's milk.

Weaning Jackson after a year of nursing was a difficult decision. The day came, however, when it was time for him to drink milk from a cup. I hated to turn him down every time he wanted to nurse. Two full days went by before he would drink anything. When he finally did, he forgot about nursing and began to gulp milk like a champion. Now he is only happy with real whole milk. But weaning took discipline! Almost more than I could manage.

Calming your soul into a state of dependence on God also requires discipline. Our natural tendency is to trust our own ambitions, gifts, talents, abilities and earthly wisdom to make decisions.

We naturally rely heavily on ourselves to secure our destiny. Just as I had to discipline myself to offer Jackson the cup, so too must you direct yourself to the nourishment of the Lord when your soul cries out for its old dependencies. If you remain faithful to Him, sooner or later you will find nothing else will satisfy.

On what people, places, or ambitions do you tend to depend more for satisfaction than on the Lord?

_____

The Quieted Soul

Weaning requires a season of discomfort. During the two days it took to wean Jackson, he was a mess. He was uneasy, insecure, and cried continuously. Since he could not have what he feverishly desired, he thought his world was coming undone. I found that my job was not only to train him to drink but also to quiet him. He needed to be consoled. I rocked him, kept him preoccupied, and did my best to make sure he understood that all would be well. And every time he desired to nurse, I offered him a warm cup of milk.

When we begin to wean ourselves of dependence on other things, we may feel uneasy, fretful, and uncomfortable. But without the crutch of dependence on ourselves or others, it becomes easier to turn to God for comfort and spiritual nourishment.

When the psalmist's soul was in a state of unrest during the "weaning" process, he wrote: "Why are you in despair, O my soul? And [why] have you become disturbed within me? Hope in God for I shall again praise Him. [For] the help of His presence" (Ps. 42:5, NASB).

What does the psalmist say is the solution to calming one's soul (42:6)?

*hope in God - praise! Remember His greatness &
what he has done!*

We depend on what we know. When we have a trust relationship with someone, we gladly depend on him or her. Likewise, when we place our trust in God, we naturally depend on Him. The more you trust your concerns to the Lord and see Him working in your life, the more willing you will be to depend on Him in the future.

The psalmist quieted his soul by remembering what God had done. What has God done in your life that can build trust when you struggle to depend on Him?

divorce - selling house; finding apt.

List situations in which you currently need to depend on the Lord. Allow Him an opportunity to win your trust.

*what next in my Life
direction*

*For My people
have committed
a double evil:
They have
abandoned Me,
the fountain of
living water,
and dug cisterns
for themselves,
cracked cisterns
that cannot
hold water.
Jeremiah 2:13*

The Rested Soul

His soul calmed and quieted, David points out the final step of the process—rest.

Seven months since Jackson last nursed, he no longer desires milk from me. In fact, he doesn't even think about it. If he wants milk, he knows it comes from the refrigerator. He rests in his new situation. So too our souls will re-orient themselves to a new way of feeding as we accept God alone for refreshment.

If we seek fulfillment in the things of the world after a season of depending on God, we will discover that it doesn't satisfy us the way it used to. When we are thirsty we need so much more than the world can offer. But Hallelujah, God never disappoints!

———

1 W. W. Wiersbe. *The Bible Exposition Commentary* (Wheaton: Victor Books, 1996), electronic ed.

TAKE ACTION

Read Jeremiah 2:13 in the margin. When we rely on anything other than Christ, we are turning to broken cisterns. What are your cisterns that cannot hold water?

_____

_____

_____

_____

Let's ask the Lord to reveal to us what "cisterns" we need to wean ourselves from in order to rely more fully on Him. This week ask Him to help you discipline yourself through the rough stages of composing and quieting your soul.

minister to Lord before Eli

Viewer Guide
Session 2

Now the boy Samuel was ministering to the LORD before Eli. And word from the LORD was rare in those days, visions were infrequent.
—1 Samuel 3:1

Samuel was a __worshipper__.

singleminded a Heartian
Undistracted worship develops __intimacy__ with God.

increases communication

Exodus 9:1 Moses - Let people go so that worship

Things we are held captive by:

- Pharaoh of __religious boundaries__ *(in a Box)*

Matt 6:1
- Pharaoh of the __need__ to __please__! *who's applause do you want*

- Pharaoh of __comparison c̄ others__ *gifts talents abilities*
Romans 12:1

- Pharaoh of __past__ __experiences__.

- Pharaoh of __Sin__ *Is. 59:2*

Isaiah 43: 18-19

Cleanse Not Condemn

A Single-Minded Worship

I WAS IN JEANS AND A T-SHIRT. My hair was rumpled. Jackson sat comfortably on my lap as we flipped channels. Finding nothing of interest, I pushed "play" on the remote control for the VCR thinking one of his videos was in the player. Instead, an image of me on stage at a recent women's event flashed on the screen. Jackson shouted "Mommy!" and watched with enthusiasm. When I tried to turn it off, He sternly told me he wanted to watch. I said, "Jackson, you don't need to watch Mommy, she's right here" and pointed to myself. He looked at me then back at the screen and said, "No, I want that mommy!" I said, "No honey, you are sitting on Mommy's lap." He said, with a look of longing, "I want that mommy." He desired the generated version of me he saw on the screen and was missing out on the real deal who was available to him all along.

Isn't that the way we can be with God? We are easily distracted by the ideas we have of Him and the picture we have generated of who He is and what He likes. It's time for us to know and accept who He really is: His true glory, character, and priorities. We need to know what He really desires so we can be in intimate relationship with Him.

DAY 1
His Glory

DAILY BREAD

The appearance of the Lord's glory to the Israelites was like a consuming fire on the mountaintop.
Exodus 24:17

True undistracted worship begins when we concentrate on His glory. The term *glory* comes from the Hebrew word *kabowd*, meaning abundance, riches, honor, dignity, splendor, and reputation. To give God glory means to ascribe to Him due honor. When we do this, we take our focus off ourselves, training our eyes on Him. God chooses to speak to those focused on His glory.

In Exodus 3 we read of Moses tending his sheep in the wilderness of Horeb. There an angel of the Lord appears in the midst of a blazing bush miraculously unconsumed by flame. Today we'll explore each of the following lessons I see reflected in the passage.

- God's glory is all around us, even in the desert places.
- God's glory exceeds comprehension.
- God's glory is reserved for only One.
- God's glory demands a response.

God's Glory Appears Even and Especially in the Desert Places

Moses spent his first 40 years as a prince in Pharaoh's court (see Ex. 2:1-10). Can you imagine how different shepherding sheep in the wilderness must have been from the luxury of Pharaoh's kingdom? Moses probably much preferred the kingdom and its comfort. Yet at the ripe age of 80, he encountered the glory of God not in a lavish palace, but in a barren desert. Often we see God's glory best against the contrast of life's dry seasons.

If you are currently in a "wilderness season," how is God using this time to reveal Himself to you? If not now, how has God used such a season in your past?

_____

_____

God's glory discovers us where we are. Moses illustrates this point well. Shepherding was beneath Moses' educational and economic expectations; he was reared as a royal, but for 40 years this prince chased sheep. Moses accepted this situation and served where he was, then God's glory showed up. My sister, be faithful even in the desert seasons, because that's where God's glory often appears.

God's Glory Exceeds Comprehension

Moses could not understand why the fiery bush was unconsumed. The sight defied the laws of nature, but Moses soon learned that God's glory is always beyond human understanding. Any attempt to comprehend His complexities or to liken Him to man minimizes His greatness and power.

What does Deuteronomy 5:8 call human attempts to capture God's glory?
☐ acceptable worship   ☒ idol-making   ☐ creativity

In Romans 1:22-25, how does God respond to man's attempt to "humanize" Him?

gave them over for the sinful desires of their heart.

As a matter of contrast, match the Scripture passage below with the appropriate illustration of God's incomparable power.

_c_ 1 Thessalonians 1:9   a. Great King; above all gods
_b_ Zechariah 4:14   b. Lord of the whole earth
_d_ Jeremiah 10:16   c. living and true God
_a_ Psalm 95:3   d. the One who formed all things *(including Israel / His tribe)*
_e_ Jude 25   e. our God; our Savior

God and His glory cannot be confined. We can only point to the glory shown in the visible signs God gives us. We must accept that He is beyond our understanding.

God's Glory Is Reserved for Only One

Fire in a dry country like Horeb could quickly spread. Moses may have been amazed not simply because the bush wasn't consumed but because only one bush burned. In this singular burning I see a hint of another important truth taught in Scripture: God does not share His glory. Even as Christians, we often desire "glory" in the eyes of man. We perform and seek attention. We want the fire reserved for God to spread to us.

What ways can you identify that you've sought to share in God's glory?

people pleasing

afirmations from man

I will act for My own sake, indeed, My own, for how can I be defiled? I will not give My glory to another.
Isaiah 48:11

What happened when you tried to share the glory reserved for God?

disappointment – no satisfying

Reflect on Isaiah 48:11 and 2 Thessalonians 2:14 in the margin. In what sense do you think God will not share His glory? In what sense does He share? Plan to discuss your answers in your group this week.

will not share His glory *it belongs to Go*
alone – He gives His glory

shares His glory *we to a share ī*
Christ the glory that is only Gods

He called you to salvation when we told you the Good News; now you can share in the glory of our Lord Jesus Christ.
2 Thessalonians 2:14, NLT

God's Glory Demands a Response

When God's glory showed up, Moses stopped his normal duties to respond. The revealed glory of God demands that we pause, listen, and heed His voice. Who knows what we miss when we don't change our plans for His? In encountering God's glory, Moses received instructions for the next phase of his life.

What three things did Moses do in response to God's glory (Ex. 3:3,5-6)?

go see strange thing; take off sandles → Holy ground
hide face → fear

How do you usually respond to God's glory?
❑ I stop what I'm doing and fall on my face.
❑ I am so busy I don't take time to notice.
❑ I really don't remember a time when God's glory showed up.
❑ Other _____

When God displays His glory to us and we know we are in His presence, we must quickly and reverently adopt three responses.

First, we must look to God (v. 3). The NASB says that Moses, when met with the sight of the burning bush, "turned aside to look" (Ex. 3:4). God's glory demands that we come away from whatever we are doing and delight in Him (Ps. 46:10).

 # 1

Second, we must humble ourselves before Him, recognizing our utter defilement before the Holy One. In verse 4, God tells Moses to remove his sandals. By removing his shoes, Moses acknowledges his unworthiness to stand in the presence of God's holiness.

 # 2

Read about Isaiah's encounter with God in Isaiah 6:1-5. In what sense did Isaiah "remove His sandals" when he saw the Lord's glory?

Woe - I'm ruined - acknowledge sin → unclean

Before the Lord delivered His message, Moses took a third and final action: He hid his face.

According to Exodus 3:6, what emotion sparked this response?

fear ·   reverence + awe

Moses wasn't afraid of God. The fear he experienced and reacted to was a reverence and awe of God. After seeing the Lord's glory and hearing His voice, Moses chose the only correct response: he hid his face. We too should bow before God's glory.

TAKE ACTION

When we worship, recognize, and respond to God's glory, we put ourselves in a position for Him to speak. Look carefully at Exodus 3:4. God spoke to Moses only after he "turned aside." God waited until he saw that Moses was enamored with His glory before giving him clear directions. I shudder to think of the times I may have missed the clear direction of God because I refused to turn aside and look.

How is God calling you to "turn aside" as a result of today's study?

_____

_____

Pray the Lord will open your spiritual eyes, revealing Himself to you as you grow in sensitivity to His leading. Make a commitment to respond to God's glory whenever you encounter it.

DAY 2
His Priorities

To worship God appropriately we've seen that we must respond to His glory. Just as essential, we must also focus on His priorities.

When God spoke from the bush in Exodus 3:5, what two things did God tell Moses to do?

- ☒ remove his shoes
- ☒ come no closer
- ❏ sing praises
- ❏ wash his hands

According to this verse, why must these things be done?

_____ standing on holy ground _____

What conclusion can you draw from this passage about requirements for approaching God? (Circle all that apply.)

respect   fear   reverence

submission   unworthiness   acceptance

In Moses' day removing shoes was what taking off a hat is now, a token of respect and submission. We are to approach God with reverence and awe. Just as He did with Moses, God gives us instructions on how to respond to His glory. We must focus on His priorities if we are to offer Him acceptable worship.

In Exodus 25-26 God told Moses exactly how to construct a tabernacle of worship where He would meet with the people. God required the tabernacle be built by specific people, who followed specific instructions, for a specific purpose. Let's take a closer look at these elements.

A Specific People

In Exodus 25:2, God specifies who will construct His tabernacle. First, they had to be His people (Deut. 7:6). Second, God specified only those "whose hearts are stirred" to participate in this project (Ex. 25:2). God receives worship from His people alone. Acceptable worship of God must be from His children who are willingly present and centered on Him. The Israelites were such a people.

> Read the following passages and explain how the relationship we have with God today parallels the relationship God had with Israel.
>
> Romans 8:15 _receive spirit of sonship (His people)_
>
> Galatians 4:5 _full rights as son — His people_

According to Exodus 36:3, the Israelites continued to bring freewill offerings morning after morning. They brought the gifts as an expression of worship and gratitude to God. We as sons and daughters of God are chosen to live as His children for all eternity. That fact should so overwhelm us with thanksgiving that we long to worship Him.

A Specific Plan

My sister, Chrystal, is a planner. She thinks ahead about everything, clipping coupons and planning shopping with the precision of a military invasion. To make it even more difficult to compete, she is a great cook who manages a budget well.

> Think through a typical week. What do you plan ahead of time?
>
> _meals parents. bible study classes_

> What does planning reveal about the level of significance you place on these things?
>
>
> _very significant_

Exodus 25–27 reveals the attention to detail God required of Moses and the Israelites. God gave specific instructions not only for the tabernacle itself but also the furniture, linens, curtains, pillars, beams, and decor. Imagine the time and patience required to meet each specification. Everything had be done correctly.

"Make this tabernacle and all its furnishings exactly like the pattern I will show you."
Exodus 25:9, NIV

Read Exodus 25:9 in the margin. Underline the word that shows how important it was that the people follow God's plans for building the tabernacle.

God considers preparing for worship important. He speaks to those who follow His instructions. This doesn't mean that He gives us a specific plan for worship or a picture of exactly how that worship should look, as He did in the building of the tabernacle. Instead, He instructs us in how to plan for opportunities to worship Him. Of course we have to turn that planning into action.

After the birth of her second child, my friend Shundria took up running with aspirations to run a marathon. To prepare, she joined a group and worked with a trainer. He gave them a running schedule, but Shundria had to implement it. Just as God gave Israel a plan to follow, God gives us a plan. But we must prepare ourselves to complete it.

What more can you do to plan and prepare yourself to spend time with God, both individually and within your local church?

Individually: _____

Corporately: _become more involved_____

A Specific Purpose

God had a purpose for the temple. He wanted to provide His people with a holy place which symbolized His presence with them—a place where He could "dwell among them" (Ex. 25:8). He even went a step further in verse 22 and said He would speak to them in that place. At all the high points of their history, the Israelites held that temple in high esteem because it was the place God manifested Himself in their midst and made His will known.

God clearly showed them a worthy purpose to all of their planning, preparation, and patience. In taking His instructions and priorities seriously, they would be invited into His very presence.

Recently my home church leadership sought to make changes. Our pastor explained that the goal was to bring God honor and invite His presence to powerfully move in our fellowship. One Sunday the pastor made a statement I will never forget. He said, "A focus on divine order always precedes an infilling of His divine presence." When we want God to show up and reveal Himself to us we have to plan and prepare to place priority on the things that are important to Him.

How much preparation do you usually put into your worship? Respond by placing a *C* for church or corporate worship and a *P* for personal worship on the continuum below.

•................................. *C* •................................. *P* ......•

just show up   *prepare prayerfully*

TAKE ACTION

Like the specific details God outlined for the children of Israel, several key things must be in place for our worship to be acceptable to Him.

Review the day by filling in the blanks below.

cleanse from sin / *forgive sin* / *repentance* must take place before we can truly worship. (1 Sam. 15:25; Ps. 51:2)

The Lord desires *glory due His name* and *worship*. (1 Chron. 16:29)

We must not worship any other *God (idol)* / *alien gods or foreign God* (Ex. 34:14; Ps. 81:9)

We must *bow down* / *kneel* in true worship. (Ps. 95:6) *reverence*

We must worship in *spirit* and in *truth* (John 4:24)

Ask the Lord to make you a true worshiper, focused on His priorities. Confess any lack of planning, preparation, or patience. Make a commitment to work on those areas. When you do, you can bank on His promise to show up and "dwell in your midst" as He did with the children of Israel.

DAY 3
His Attributes

To worship God acceptably we must know Him. Understanding God's attributes—the distinguishing marks of His character—will help us grow to appreciate Him in a deeper, more intimate way. Meditating on His attributes helps us move from knowing *about* God to truly *knowing* Him. Daniel 11:32 tells us, "The people who know their God will be strong."

DAILY BREAD

"I am the God of your father, the God of Abraham, the God of Isaac, and the God of Jacob."
Exodus 3:6

What parts of God's reputation were revealed to Moses in Exodus 3:6?

Faithfulness

God reminded Moses of His record of faithfulness, so Moses knew he could count on God regardless of circumstances. Likewise, no matter how you feel or what you experience, God's attributes remain true. His perfection sets Him apart from all others. That knowledge should drive us to our knees in true worship.

We cannot capture in one day everything God's nature encompasses. However, we can look at some of God's attributes clearly outlined in Scripture.

Look carefully at the list in the margin. Which of God's attributes have you seen most evidenced in or impacting your life?

Love, merciful, goodness

- He is just. Hebrews 10:30-31
- He is good. Matthew 19:17
- He is holy. Revelation 15:4
- He is righteous. Psalm 119:137
- He is sovereign. Isaiah 46:9-10
- He is everywhere. Ezekiel 48:35
- He is all knowing. Hebrews 4:13
- He is unchanging. James 1:17
- He is truth. Isaiah 65:16
- He is merciful. Ephesians 2:4
- He is jealous. Exodus 34:14
- He is love. 1 John 4:8
- He is eternal. Isaiah 48:12
- He is a provider. Genesis 22:14
- He is a healer. Exodus 15:26

When God Reveals His Attributes

We've followed Moses into the desert where God revealed His glory, outlined His plan, and gave Moses specific instructions. Let's see how Moses responded to the attributes of God.

What does Moses' response to God in Exodus 3:11 and 4:10 indicate about his feelings?

lack of trust, faith

Moses had indeed encountered God and heard God's voice, but he needed to experience His power.

Consider the tasks that God has called you to do. How do you feel about yourself in relation to those instructions?
❑ fully able ❑ somewhat prepared ❑ ill-equipped

As I read Exodus I discover that Moses remained dependent on God throughout his service to the Lord. Because he felt ill-equipped, he never thought he had arrived. Moses remained aware of his own desperate need. In Exodus 33:18 Moses begs God, "Please, let me see Your glory." The Lord's response appears in verses 19-23.

Read Exodus 33:19-23. Which of God's attributes are mentioned in these verses?

goodness, mercy, love (compassion) Holiness

God controlled how much of His glory Moses witnessed (v. 20-22). No matter what you think you need from God, He knows what is best for you. He controls how He meets you and what He chooses to reveal about Himself.

You may feel you need His healing touch, while He may decide to reveal His peace in the midst of your ailing body. You may think you need His financial provision, and He may decide you need to learn dependence. He knows what's best and will reveal the attributes we need in His timing.

Now let's look at the specific attributes God chose to reveal to Moses.

The Power of God

When God replaced the broken tablets of the law, He began revealing Himself to Moses by reminding him of His great power (see Ex. 34:5-7). The word order in Hebrew in Exodus 34:6 appears this way, "The Lord, the Lord God" (NASB). The Lord God means "mighty God or powerful One."

According to Exodus 14:9 and 32:7-8 what are some of the reasons Moses needed to be reminded of God's might?

The people he lead - had turned away - discouraged enemy pursuing

With the people's great sin of creating and worshiping a golden calf fresh on his mind, Moses likely needed a reminder that God is great enough not only to defeat their enemies but also to forgive their iniquity! God's power and might are so great that they powerfully and fully cleanse us of iniquity. Second Corinthians 12:9 says, "His grace is sufficient for you."

How does the truth that God can forgive because of His grace and almighty power make you feel?

sometime shame guilt but also Hope

The Mercy of God

God revealed His mercy to Moses through the words *compassionate* (merciful) and gracious, slow to anger and abounding in loving-kindness and forgiveness (Ex. 34:6-7). This is significant because God reminded Moses of His grace as Moses stood to represent the people of Israel, confess their sins, and seek forgiveness before receiving the second installment of the Ten Commandments.

God showed the attribute of His mercy before revealing the law. Why might a reminder of God's mercy be important before receiving the law?

Law - expose sin - needed a compassionate God

God wanted to assure Moses that His mercy could extend to the children of Israel who had grumbled, rebelled, and erected idols against Him. God forgives sin, and He reminded Moses that no one is beyond His forgiveness. God never gives law without buffering it with grace. In the midst of our sin, His mercy steps in and saves us from ourselves.

Justice - guilty will not go unpunished → harsher aspect of nature

The Justice of God

> **God never gives law without buffering it with grace.**

In Exodus 34:7 God also reveals His justice: "He will not leave the guilty unpunished." After establishing His mercy, God reveals to Moses a harsher aspect of His nature: He is a God of truth and judgment. Although we know the wonders of His grace and mercy, we must not take His justice lightly. Knowledge of His mercy should not lead us to take advantage of it but should lead us to repentance (Rom. 2:4).

Understand that sin leads to consequence. God punished the children of Israel—even to the third and fourth generation. But His grace and mercy provided forgiveness. Although He punished sin, He loved the sinners.

TAKE ACTION

Moses' response to the revelation of God's character appears in Exodus 34:8. Read the passage and answer the following.

How quickly did Moses respond? _____ *at once !* _____

What did Moses' external position show about his internal state?

_____ *bowed to worship* _____

In response to the revealed character of God, Moses worshiped. We don't know whether or not God revealed the attributes Moses felt he needed to see, but Moses' actions show us he was satisfied with what He saw of God.

Commentator Matthew Henry says Moses' desire to worship God shows:
1. He humbly revered and adored God.
2. He was joyful and thankful at His discovery of God.
3. He was submissive to the revelation of God's will.[1]

May these three things be true of us as God reveals His attributes throughout this study.

DAY 4
His Acceptance

How can we consistently hear God's voice? We must take the focus off ourselves, looking instead to His glory and priorities, meditating on His attributes. To worship God appropriately, we also need to grasp His acceptance. As long as we feel condemned, we will have difficulty hearing God speak. Today we will see how Moses got a lesson on God's acceptance.

When God spoke, Moses hid his face (Ex. 3:6). In a way, I can relate to his reaction. When LifeWay first contacted me about writing this Bible study, I was intimidated. As my husband and I left the first meeting with the publishing team, I looked at him and exclaimed, "I can't do it!" I felt ill-equipped for the task. My husband, Jerry, encouraged me to talk to the Lord before making a decision.

Through Bible study and prayer, God affirmed that I was to take the challenge. But, like Moses, I felt I could never measure up to the task. The Lord has to continuously remind me that He is in control and will accomplish good things through me. Though we, like Moses, should approach the presence of God with humility, we must not hang our heads because we feel unacceptable or inadequate. Hebrews 10 explains why as Christians we are accepted by God. We will look at portions of this chapter in today's study.

DAILY BREAD
"Be careful not to practice your righteousness in front of people, to be seen by them. Otherwise, you will have no reward from your Father in heaven."
Matthew 6:1

The Problem

List the things you like best about yourself.

_____

Every year the Jewish people celebrated the Day of Atonement. On this day, the ceremonially cleansed priests entered the holy of holies and offered sacrifices for the sin of the people. The holy of holies was a sacred room in the tabernacle: it contained the ark of the covenant and the mercy seat that signified the very presence of God (see Ex. 25:22). Only the high priest, under great scrutiny, could go into this sacred room. Each year the priests would venture into this place with fear and trembling, offering sacrifices for the sins of the people.

The problem, however, was that the priests were also humans—they too sinned. In our own power we will always be inadequate. Only God's sacrifice of His Son for our sin makes us acceptable.

Why do the traits you just listed not make you acceptable to God? (see Isa. 64:6)

we are all unclean even what we do is unrighteous

We are not made acceptable to God by *who* we are but by *Whose* we are. Jesus bridges the gap between our imperfection and His holiness (Eph. 2:8-9). Hebrews 10:14 tells us, "For by one offering He has perfected forever those who are sanctified." The word *perfect* here does not mean "without sin" but rather "perfectly adequate."[2] The death of Jesus on the cross is the only sacrifice ever needed for us to be acceptable and adequate in His sight.

> **We are not made acceptable to God by *who* we are but by *Whose* we are.**

The Israelites continuously tried to find perfection, following the law and offering sacrifices, but they always came up short. Year after year they offered the same sacrifices, but the Day of Atonement and the offering of the blood of animals for the sin of the people was basically useless. No matter how often the people sacrificed, no matter how closely they tried to follow the law, they remained unacceptable to God.

In what ways have you, like the Old Testament saints, tried following the law to make yourself acceptable to God?

☑ a moral lifestyle ☐ religious activity ☑ prayer
☐ sacrificial giving ☑ confession ☐ other _____

Hear this incredibly liberating truth: you cannot make yourself acceptable to God. Hebrews 10:1-4 explains that the continued offering of bull and goat blood did not take away sins. You can be sure that whatever you are offering will not "perfect" you either.

The Solution

In the margin, list the things you like least about yourself.

Jesus is the Son of God. He makes us acceptable to God and gives us the right to claim God as our Father. As God's adopted children, we each become "co-heirs with Christ" (Rom. 8:17). We become sons and daughters to God (2 Cor. 6:18).

How thankful I am to live on this side of the cross! By receiving the gift of salvation and because of Jesus' blood we are forever accepted by God. We have a sure guarantee of our position with God—being right with God and living in relationship with Him forever.

According to Ephesians 2:6 what is our position once we become Christians?

raised up c̄ Christ; seated with him in heavenly realm

According to Hebrews 7:22, what guarantees this covenant?

Jesus - guarantees better covenant

Why does the trait you like least about yourself not keep you from a standing of righteousness before God?

_____

We no longer have to worry about our standing before God. We do not have to be concerned with whether or not He will receive our worship. By accepting the perfect sacrifice of Jesus for the remission of our sins, we can "have confidence to enter the holy place" (Heb. 10:19, NASB). The Old Testament saints did not have this right, but because of Jesus—you and I do! As Christians, we are completely acceptable to God. Nothing can change our standing before Him!

TAKE ACTION

Because God accepts us in Christ, we can approach God's throne with confidence (see Heb. 4:16). If you aren't certain you have received God's gift of eternal life, read the information that follows. If you already have a personal relationship with the Lord, spend some time in prayer, thanking Him for your salvation.

A relationship with God begins by admitting we are not perfect and continue to fall short of God's standards. Romans 3:23 says, "All have sinned and fall short of the glory of God." The price for these wrongdoings is separation from God. But God provided a way to get rid of that separation by coming down to earth in the form of Jesus. When Jesus was crucified on the cross He provided a way to allow our sins to be forgiven and restore our relationship with God. God doesn't ask us to clean up our lives before we come to Him. He wants us to come as we are, receiving Him as Savior and Lord.

Forgiveness begins when we admit our sin to God. When we do, He will forgive us and restore our relationship with Him. "If we confess our sins, He is faithful and righteous to forgive us our sins and to cleanse us from all unrighteousness" (1 John 1:9).

This love gift and relationship with God is not just for a special few but for everyone. "Everyone who calls on the name of the Lord will be saved" (Rom. 10:13).

If you want a personal relationship with the Lord, pray this prayer:

Jesus, I am sorry for the things I have done wrong. I thank You for dying on a cross for me. I am willing to turn away from anything that displeases You in my life and from this day on I want to live my life Your way. I invite You to come into my life now and make me a new person. Thank You, Jesus.

If you just prayed this prayer, share your experience with your small-group facilitator, someone in your group, your pastor, or a trusted Christian friend. Continue to grow in your new relationship through reading the Bible, talking to God through prayer, and fellowshipping with other Christians. Welcome to God's family!

DAY 5
His Approval

DAILY BREAD

So Jesus has also become the guarantee of a better covenant.
Hebrews 7:22

January of 2003 marked our son Jackson's dedication service. I had everything planned down to the last detail. I color-coordinated my family's clothing. For several weeks I clothed little Jackson in several of his cutest outfits and parted his hair on one side and then the other, mentally gauging which combination I liked best. Everything was perfect. The morning of the event was filled with hustle and bustle as we prepared for the dedication service. We were so excited as we made our way to the church that beautiful Sunday morning. My baby adorable, my husband handsome, and my ensemble flawless, it seemed everything was prepared. Before thousands of people, my son would be presented to the church for the first time.

As we drove to the church, a weight hit my spirit like a ton of bricks. In planning my son's event, I had remembered every detail except the most important: the Lord. In my busyness, I had forgotten that the event wasn't about me or my family but about presenting Jackson to Him. Embarrassment and shame filled me as I realized I had been more concerned with external appearance than the internal significance of the morning. How could I become so consumed with pleasing the people watching instead of pleasing God?

Focused on His Approval

Read Moses' conversation with God in Exodus 3:10-16. Here God reveals a final principle about seeking to be single-minded in our worship of Him.

What is Moses' main concern (10-11,13)?

who am I - what should I tell Him

How did God redirect Moses' attention (12,14-16)?

I will be with you : say I Am Sent you

What are you most concerned with when God gives you instructions to follow? Do you consume yourself with thoughts of what others may think of you or do you redirect your attention to what the Lord thinks?

Read Matthew 6:1-4. In this passage, Jesus instructs us how to give in His name. What motivates you to serve others?
❑ attention   ❑ friendship   ❑ the acceptance of others
❑ God's acceptance   ❑ other _____

Whom do you desire to please in those instances?

In Exodus 3:10-16 God reveals to Moses that he can carry out His instructions only if he takes his eyes off the people and keeps them on God. We must do the same. Our acts must be dedicated to God alone—not to the approval of others.

Does your personality lend itself to a desire to please others? ☒ yes ❏ no ❏ I'm not sure. If so, how does that desire manifest itself?

deny self - No voice - I don't care -

Describe a time when you did something "religious" to satisfy people more than to please God.

Won Ben board

While external appearance or actions may consume us, our internal motivation concerns God. Appearing to be holy has no kingdom value.

The Pharisees and scribes were religiously upstanding men. They sought notice by their ceremonial washings, fasting, prayer, and giving alms. They were highly respected for their seemingly extreme obedience of the law. Yet Jesus opposed no group more passionately and visibly than He did these religious leaders. It neither mattered how impeccable their actions seemed nor how holy their behavior appeared; Christ was not impressed. *✓ pure motives of heart*

Read Jesus' words to the Pharisees in Matthew 23:23-29. Paraphrase verses 25 and 26.

Teacher of the Law - display themselves for show looking Godly but far from it.

How does it feel to be clean on the outside but dirty on the inside? We need to take close inventory of our hearts to make sure the motives behind our actions are pure. God responds to those who seek Him with their whole hearts. I believe those who single-mindedly focus on gaining His approval will clearly worship Him and pave the way to hear His voice.

Read John 4:22-24 in the margin. Underline key words that describe the type of worshiper God seeks.

Ask the Lord to help you offer Him the authentic worship He desires.

You worship guessing in the dark; we Jews worship in the clear light of day. God's way of salvation is made available through the Jews. But the time is coming— it has, in fact, come—when what you're called will not matter and where you go to worship will not matter. God is sheer being itself— Spirit. Those who worship him must do it out of their very being, their spirits, their true selves, in adoration.
John 4:22-24, The Message

The Heart of the Matter

Deuteronomy 4:29 says that when we search for the Lord with all of our hearts we will find Him. So what keeps us from seeing His face and clearly hearing His voice? Maybe our hearts are at the core of the problem. God seeks passionate followers who love Him passionately. He doesn't care about our religious activity, only that our actions are rooted in love for Him.

God seeks passionate followers who love Him passionately.

To be single-minded in our search for God, our hearts cannot be caught up in details that steal attention from Him. Maybe we don't find Him and hear His voice clearly because our attention is divided. Instead of being consumed with gaining His approval, we are distracted by the lure of other's acceptance.

TAKE ACTION

The Lord is not impressed with our seemingly religious involvement and half-hearted approach to worship. He is concerned with whether our search for Him finds root in our hearts. He promises that when our hearts are focused on seeking Him, we will find Him.

What has God specifically spoken to you about this week?

silence – be quiet before him

Write at least one thing you can do to focus on each area we've considered this week:

His glory _It belongs to God_

His priorities _My heart – my devotion – center on Him_

His attributes _Know them. He can do them_

His acceptance _He loves me! unconditionally_

His approval _focus on him – not approval of others_

Turn your responses into a prayer. After talking to the Lord about your goals, write today's date in the margin to remind you of your renewed commitment to focus on Him in worship.

---

1 Matthew Henry, *Matthew Henry's Commentary on the Whole Bible* (Peabody: Hendrickson, 1996), electronic ed.

2 *New International Version Disciple's Study Bible* (Nashville: Holman Bible Publishers, 1998), 1587.

Set apart decision

Now the boy Samuel was ministering to the LORD before Eli. And **word from the LORD was rare in those days, visions were infrequent**.
—1 Samuel 3:1

Samuel was ___*set*___ ___*apart*___ (*from crowd*) *different*

set apart = ___*Sanctified*___ and ___*holy*___
process become more like Christ

Sin provokes God to ___*withhold*___ His word.
sin in life – can't hear God

Three stages of sanctification.

1. ___*positional*___ sanctification
2. ___*Lifestyle*___ sanctification *Choose to live to Spirit free from power of Sin*
3. ___*Ultimate*___ sanctification *free from presence of sin*

1. Remember the ___*promises*___ 2 Cor 6: 16-17
   The Promise of ___*Fellowship c̄ God*___
   The Promise of ___*Relationship*___ c̄ God.

2. Remove the ___*Baggage*___ *contaminate body spirit*

   2 Cor 7: 1 – Sanctification

   Is it worth it?

Distraction – key to Satan's work

A Set-Apart Holiness

IN 1956, A SAVAGE INDIAN MAN nicknamed "Grandfather" participated in the killings of Jim Elliot and several other missionaries in Ecuador. In 2001 I met Grandfather and my life was impacted forever. He shared how drastically his life had changed since 1956. The Lord was now his Savior and he and his tribesmen were serving Christ. Now they were sons and daughters of a King and they were living a life that spoke of their new identity in the Lord. He explained that his visit to America had been alarming. He was shocked at how Christians in America seem to so closely resemble the rest of society. He was dismayed by how we didn't seem to be living in a way that would clearly show we served a different God.

As we all sat pinned to our seats with conviction it occurred to us that we had not just been saved to spend eternity with Christ but to live for Him while we are in history. Like the savage Indians changed by a relationship with Christ, we must choose to live a lifestyle of sanctification that sets us apart from the world and speaks of a relationship with our great God.

DAY 1
Dead to Sin

The Bible uses several terms to describe the process of putting ourselves in a position to hear from God. This week we'll look at one of the most prominent, the word sanctification. If you were able to join us for our video session together you'll recall the discussion of the three stages of this process.

Match the three stages of sanctification to the two sets of corresponding descriptions by writing the numbers in the blanks.

_2_ Freedom from the power of sin
_3_ Freedom from the presence of sin
_1_ Freedom from the penalty of sin

1. Positional sanctification
2. Lifestyle sanctification *(progressional)*
3. Ultimate sanctification

_3_ Upon entering heaven
_2_ During the Christian walk on earth
_1_ At the moment of salvation

As Christians we are sanctified—set apart or made holy. Positionally this process was accomplished by the sacrifice of Christ on the cross. When we enter into a personal relationship with Jesus, the punishment for our sins has already been covered by His death and resurrection.

DAILY BREAD

We know that our old self was crucified with Him in order that sin's dominion over the body may be abolished, so that we may no longer be enslaved to sin, since a person who has died is freed from sin's claims.

Romans 6:6-7

Although we have been sanctified by faith in Christ, it is our responsibility to actively pursue holy lives (1 Pet. 1:15). We are set apart by God for His purposes, and everything we do reflects on Him.

Daddy always told us to remember our last name. He wanted us to act like his children, leaving people with a good impression of the family. My mother's advice, probably because I look so much like her, was even more specific: "Do not go anywhere or do anything questionable where someone might mistake you for me!"

I was always positionally "set apart" to my parents because I will always be their child. However, they also demanded that I live as a positive testimony to the Evans family name. They ensured that I knew to make wise decisions—not just for my sake but for theirs. My parents trusted me to act in a way that positively set me apart as their daughter.

As believers we've been born into the family of God, and His family name has a holy reputation. We are His children, and we must choose a lifestyle that will not jeopardize that great heritage. Daily we must make decisions that set us apart from the world. We can never perfectly uphold our divine family name on our own strength, but we can live as set apart vessels—no longer enslaved to sin—through God's power.

Since your salvation, what signs do you see that your desires have changed?

don't appreciate slanted jokes
speak truth   laziness
tought life   self desires ← food
*   drunk*

Plan to talk about these signs in your group this week.

In what specific areas might you still be living as a slave to sin?

The Process of Dying to Sin

Though as children of God we are no longer enslaved by sin, it still surrounds and entices us. Ignoring it and avoiding its allure remains a challenge—especially when a sin has become a satisfying habit.

Read 1 Corinthians 15:31-34. According to verse 31, how often did Paul find it necessary to die to his flesh?

- ❏ occasionally
- ❏ frequently
- ❏ hourly
- ✔ daily
- ❏ once
- ❏ never

As Christians we have a responsibility to *daily* die to the flesh, or let go of those things that distract us from our relationship with the Lord. For me, gluttony is a sin with which I struggle constantly. I love to eat! It makes me happy to see good food waiting for me. I am not one of those women content to order a nice, petite salad. I will not only devour my meal of meat and potatoes, but I'll scan your plate for leftovers.

God has dealt with me on this! Each day I must die to my desire to eat more than I need. I know that denying myself the extra helpings will ultimately make me a better example of how God's children should live. As I get more into the habit of sacrificing my selfish desires in this area, it becomes easier. But I suspect that gluttony will always be a struggle for me. I must remember that self control strengthens my Christian witness.

What sins do you have to crucify daily?

_____

_____

True Freedom

As we fully realize the result of dying to our sin through Christ, we move toward the abundant life promised in John 10:10. Thanks be to God that we are no longer under sin's power. Jesus set us free.

My life verse is Galatians 5:1 which says, "Christ has liberated us into freedom. Therefore stand firm and don't submit again to a yoke of slavery."

God's freedom = liberty to live as you should, not as you please.

Society's freedom = liberty to live as you please, not as you should.

Repeat this verse aloud twice using the personal pronoun "me." Write it on a card and post it on your bathroom mirror, car dashboard or somewhere you will see it often.

The world's definition of freedom often means the right to openly rebel against God. But that kind of freedom can bring a heavy price. Sexual freedom leads to guilt, sickness, fear, and unwanted pregnancy. The freedom to abuse chemical substances results in addiction and isolation. Gossip leads to distrust and broken relationships. In every case, the world's freedom ultimately leads to emptiness and despair.

God offers freedom from sin that leads to abundance and peace. A life yielded to Him results in the fruit of the Spirit: love, joy, peace, patience, kindness, goodness, faithfulness, gentleness, and self-control (Gal. 5:22-23). As Christians, we must embrace God's freedom. We must make decisions and choices that will lead us to live set apart for Him.

Based on what you read in the previous section, complete the chart below listing differences in worldly freedom and freedom in Christ. I've given you one example.

Therefore do not let sin reign in your mortal body, so that you obey its desires. And do not offer any parts of it to sin as weapons for unrighteousness. But as those who are alive from the dead, offer yourselves to God, and all the parts of yourselves to God as weapons for righteousness.
Romans 6:12-13

Worldly freedom	Freedom in Christ
Sexual promiscuity	true intimacy in marriage
mans approval (pleasing)	Gods' approval
mans justice -	Godly justice - vengence is mine
mans toughts	God centered
Self centered	

TAKE ACTION

In Romans 6:12-13 (see margin) the words *let, obey,* and *offer* are actions that require a choice. Sin seeks to carry you away from the truth that you have been set apart as a child of God. Continually dying to sin is a great challenge, but it is worth the effort. The benefits of living for God far outweigh the cost. We must ask ourselves: To what will we yield? To our flesh or to our new nature?

End today's study with prayer time. Ask God to sanctify every area of your life and to give you the strength to die to self and yield to Him. Write your prayer below.

Please set aside every area of my life as it belongs to you - Show me areas where I need to decrease (areas where "I still rule) May I be a living sacrifice as I offer you every part of me

DAY 2
Alive in Christ

DAILY BREAD

"What is the surpassing greatness of His power toward us who believe. These are in accordance with the working of the strength of His might which He brought about in Christ, when He raised Him from the dead and seated Him at His right hand in the heavenly places."
Ephesians 1:19-20, NASB

Popular trends often provide a window into the souls of people within a culture, revealing inner desires such as the drive for acceptance, fame, and power. The fantasy of Hollywood movies often reveals what people really want. An awkward youth gets bitten by a radioactive spider and gains superhuman abilities. A troubled young man seeks to avenge the murder of his parents by dressing in a bat costume. The X-men display superhuman qualities. Like these fictional characters, we often feel the need to be more than we are—perhaps that's why we are so drawn to superheroes.

In what specific areas of your life do you wish you could run into a phone booth and come out with the extra power to meet the demands of life?

_____

God has provided something even better for Christians. Romans 6:5 tells us that since we have been united with Christ in His death, we can be assured that the same power that raised Him from the dead is available to us. His death and resurrection unite us with Him. You can live a sanctified life because you have divine power.

Ephesians 2:6 says we have been raised with Christ. Most Christians consider this a past accomplishment. In Philippians 3:10, however, Paul wrote that one of his greatest aspirations was to actively *know* the power of Christ's resurrection. He wanted to grasp that power, using it to live free of sin's grip. As Christians we have access to this power that brought Jesus out of the grave.

Yesterday we considered that we are sanctified by having died to sin through Christ. We also discussed the importance of daily dying to sin as we live our lives for Him, but lifestyle sanctification doesn't stop there. We must be set apart *from* one thing and set apart *to* something else.

On the chart below, list what Colossians 3:8,12-14 tells us to put off and what we must put on as Christ's followers. *forbearance - forgiveness*

Put Off	Put On
anger	compassion
rage	kindness
malice	humility
slander	gentleness
filthy language	patience
lies	love

Which items in the list would be most difficult for you to put off? Why?

_____

_____

Which would be most difficult to put on and why?

_____

_____

I pray that the eyes of your heart may be enlightened so you may know what is the hope of His calling, what are the glorious riches of His inheritance among the saints.
Ephesians 1:18

Paul's knows his request is not easy. That's why in Ephesians 1:18 he prays that we will know the great riches we received in Christ (see margin). He wants us to know that our position as God's children means more than just salvation from sin. We also have an inheritance to claim here on earth—including the same power which resurrected Christ from the dead. How unfortunate that many believers never acknowledge their inheritance or experience its joy.

Paul further describes this inheritance in Ephesians 1:19-20. In doing so he refers to three distinct elements. We receive an incomparable power, a superhuman power, and an overcoming power.

An Incomparable Power

In Ephesians 1:19 Paul describes the power at work in believers with a three-word Greek phrase: *hyperballo megethos dunamis*. The NIV translates them: "incomparably great power." The apostle used strong words to describe the spiritual force living inside us, empowering us to "put on" those things we need.

To whom is the "surpassing greatness of His power" directed in Ephesians 1:19?
- ❏ the whole world
- ☒ all believers
- ☒ obedient saints
- ❏ lost people

The power to live righteously comes from the Holy Spirit, a living force given only to believers. According to Romans 8:9-10, if you are a believer, the Holy Spirit is living in you, giving you the power to live a sanctified life.

Humility, forgiveness, gentleness, and patience: these are indeed impossibilities in your own strength. Without allowing the Holy Spirit to daily work in your life, you cannot be patient on your job or with your family. You cannot be loving when others are not loving towards you. You cannot put aside anger and resentment when you feel they are deserved. You need His power to make this happen. Thank God for the Holy Spirit who enables us to carry out the Father's will. Without His intervention, living righteously is impossible.

Fill in the chart below, illustrating the difference the Spirit's power makes in your life. I have given you an example to start.

Without the Spirit's incomparable power	With the Spirit's Incomparable Power
I get fed up with my kids.	I patiently respond to them.
love for others *do not know the truth* *over come – defeated*	*love others more* *knowledg. wisdom* *ability follow thord*

A Superhuman Power

The second phrase in Ephesians 1:19 which begs further study is "the working." The Greek word for *working* is *energien,* which reminds me of the English word "energy." Not surprisingly, it means "energetic power."[1] Scripture uses *energien* only to reference superhuman power. While *dunamis* power comes from the indwelling of the Holy Spirit, the *energien* to use that power is a superhuman phenomenon.

Simply by being born again through salvation in Christ, we have the Holy Spirit's *dunamis* power residing in us, but our inheritance also includes the energy to get us up and into action so that this great power can be used.

Which is more difficult for you?
❏ believing God has given you the power to serve Him
☒ actually getting up and doing what God has called you to do

Do you currently lack the spiritual energy required to accomplish something God asks of you? ❏ yes ❏ no ☒ I'm not sure.
If yes, describe the situation in the margin.

An Overcoming Power

In Ephesians 1:19 the third phrase that begs attention is "the strength of His might." The Greek word for *strength* here is *kratos.* It means "power that overcomes resistance" or "dominion." This term is used only of God, never of humans.

The Greek word used for *might* in this passage is *ischus,* meaning "powerful ability." Paul says that God has a "powerful ability to take dominion" over anything. Interestingly, this is the same power that He used to take dominion over death and the same power that placed Jesus Christ in a position of dominion over "every ruler and authority, power and dominion, and every title given, not only in this age but also in the one to come" (v. 21). This same power helps us overcome sin in our lives and live in victory.

Paul wants us to know that we have access to God's power; therefore, we no longer have an excuse not to put on righteousness. The apostle realized that Christians would lack the ability to live for Christ, so he reminded us that the power available to us comes through God's strength—not our own. We must ask God to help us live sanctified lives through His dynamic and divine power.

Match the words describing God's power with their definitions.

   C 1. dunamis   a. the strength to get up and use the power God has given

   a 2. energien   b. the power to overcome the resistance

   b 3. kratos   c. the raw power supplied by the Spirit to every believer

TAKE ACTION

Pretend you are explaining Philippians 2:13 to a friend. What would you say about the source of our power to serve Christ? Write your response, including the concepts of *dunamis*, *energien*, and *kratos*.

                       (dunamis)

When we believe we receive power that works in us

The (energien) power to act out his purposes and the power full will to over come resistance

Remember, sanctification means dying to sin but it also means living to Christ, We don't just stop sinning. We will always struggle with sin in this life. However, we can put on Christ, allowing His power to flow through us, His energy to motivate us, and His strength to rule over and through us. In one sense we have put on Christ once-for-all. In another sense we must put on Christ daily.

We began today discussing the longing in our hearts to be something more than we are. How does Christ living through you answer and even exceed that need?

encourages me be more intimate t him - contemplative prayer.

DAY 3
A Firm Decision

DAILY BREAD

"If it doesn't please you to worship the LORD, choose for yourselves today the one you will worship: the gods your fathers worshiped beyond the Euphrates River, or the gods of the Amorites in whose land you are living. As for me and my family, we will worship the LORD."
Joshua 24:15

When most of us read phrases like "die to self" and "allow Christ to live through you," we are tempted to ignore the implications these words have on our responsibility as Christians. In fact, if we are painfully honest, I suspect we would like to "cut corners" when it comes to living a sanctified life. Subconsciously we ask ourselves, "What can I do to 'just get by' as a Christian?" Then we mentally assure ourselves that being lukewarm and riding the fence in our Christianity is OK.

I think Romans 6:12-13, as presented in *The Message*, best addresses this issue: "You must not give sin a vote in the way you conduct your lives. Don't give it the time of day. Don't even run little errands that are connected with that old way of life. Throw yourselves wholeheartedly and full time—remember, you've been raised from the dead—into God's way of doing things."

As I begin writing today's study, I am trembling. Already I feel the Holy Spirit's conviction welling up inside of me, reminding me of ways I've compromised my devotion to the Lord and taken the easy road. I know that I'm sometimes guilty of "giving sin a vote," allowing the flesh to direct how I act and what I say. For instance, I've let pride prevent me from speaking to others about the Lord. I've also allowed jealousy or bitterness to affect my relationships. But I must not allow sin to influence my decisions. I am a child of God. I must give God His rightful place as Master of my life.

In what ways have you "run little errands" that connect you with your old lifestyle?

dating; not speaking up — I have something to say

In Joshua 24, Joshua calls the people to make a clear choice between serving other gods or serving the Lord. In essence he says: "Stop riding the fence! Mediocre devotion to God is unacceptable. Make a decision to follow Him wholeheartedly, and make it this very day" (vv. 14-15).

I suspect most of us have chosen to serve the Lord once or many times. Yet we still struggle to lead a life without compromise. Let's see if the process Joshua describes can help us with this life challenge.

Incentives for Commitment

Joshua challenged the people to make a clear choice between their idols and the Lord. Perhaps to emphasize the significance of God's challenge, Joshua began by gathering the people at Shechem.

compromise devotion

mediocre devotion

— great tree of Moreh

spiritual experience

What happened at Shechem (Gen. 12:7) that would make this location significant to the children of Israel?

Lord appeared to Abram — to your offspring
I will give this land

Often, in order to get our attention, God takes us back to a place where He made a promise to us, showed us His power, or revealed Himself to us. He may even take us back to a painful place, using it to remind us to serve Him whole-heartedly. In this sense, we all have our Shechems.

Your Shechem may not be a physical location. It may be an emotional or mental state. For instance, the Lord might bring an emotional Shechem to your memory, reminding you of a painful relationship in your past. He shows you again how that relationship affected you and the decisions you made as a result. Going back to this place reminds you of His goodness, grace, and power. Our Shechems teach us to seek God's face, reminding us of what an intimate relationship with Him really means.

What Shechems, painful or joyful, has God used to remind you that He alone is Lord and is able to lead you and love you through life's trials?

relation ē Skip — old dating ways
versus a new creation – wanted love
fell into old pattern — giving in a role!

Don't forget the lessons learned at your Shechem. God uses them to guide us into the future.

After Joshua assembled the leaders at Shechem and reminded them of God's goodness to them in the past, he challenged them to faithfulness. Joshua provided four reasons the children of Israel should willingly and uncompromisingly surrender to God. Let's consider the first two today and look at the other two tomorrow.

1. Remember the Call

Read Joshua 24:2. Joshua begins by reminding the people of Abraham's background and call. According to this verse what did the Israelite forefathers, namely Abraham's, do?

☑ committed themselves to God   ☑ worshiped other gods
❑ feared God   ❑ ran from God

Abram, later to be called friend of God (see Isa. 41:8) and listed as an honoree in the great hall of faith (see Heb. 11), had a legacy of idol worship. Only the call of God could extract him from idol-worshipers and make him a covenant-keeper.

"This is what the LORD, the God of Israel, says: 'Long ago your ancestors, including Terah, the father of Abraham and Nahor, lived beyond the Euphrates River and worshiped other gods.'"
Joshua 24:2

Notice Abraham's past didn't disqualify Him from being called by God and used for His service. Likewise, your past—no matter how sinful—cannot remove you from the reach of God's calling. The same God who called Abraham has also called you with a holy calling (1 Tim. 1:9). He calls us to spiritually die to our sins that we might live new lives in Him.

Circle three things God called Abraham to leave (see Gen. 12:1).

relatives   occupation   children
land   false gods   his father's house

God desired to do wonderful things for His kingdom through Abraham and so he called him away from his past lifestyle and everything that accompanied it.

Abraham had a choice. He could either follow God or remain with those things that would pull him back into his former, idolatrous lifestyle. Would he stay with His family, friends, and gods or would he venture—on faith—to a land the one true God would show Him?

To move into the calling the Lord has for us, we must willingly leave some things behind. God will not share our time and attention with other gods. Anything or anybody that receives more of my worship than God does is an idol, including television, books, the internet, or even a relationship. Even necessary and good things like food and sleep can become idols if they become more important than God. God will not share us with anything or anyone that takes our eyes off Him. He demands all of us.

As I write this lesson, I am so convicted by my own lukewarm service to God. I cannot begin to tell you how idols in my life have sometimes taken precedent over my allegiance to the One true God. Sometimes my mind chooses the god of television when God Himself calls me to spend time with Him. Other times, God asks me talk to Him, but I ignore Him because sleep is my desire. I've even allowed greed to overshadow the Holy Spirit's conviction to give to someone in need. How often I act like the Israelites, straddling the fence between serving God and serving my own desires! But today, as the Holy Spirit works in my heart, I renew my commitment to uncompromising and complete submission to Him. Will you?

What things is God asking you to set aside to follow Him more closely?

my own ideas of the way things are - judging

I have what you need to know — listen to me

When we consider the awesome privilege of being included in God's family, we are wise to willingly and gladly leave behind things that might hold us back from living bold, victorious lives for Him.

2. Remember the Promise

Read Joshua 24:3-4. God made a special promise to the seed of
Abraham. What was that promise? (See also Gen. 12:2-3.)

make you a great Nation — I will bless you.
your name will be great you will be a blessing

What obstacles did Abraham have to deal with in light of this promise?
(See Rom. 4:19.)

weakening of his faith
body was old - (as good as dead   100 yrs old
Sarai also old

What does Hebrews 11:12 tell you about God's faithfulness?

came descendants as numerous as
the stars in sky & countless as
sand on the seashore - Gods promises come true

You can't depend on many things in this world. Times change and
people are fickle. But you can always count on one true thing—God's
Word. If the Father decrees it then it will come to pass. In Joshua
24:3-4 God tells the children of Israel to remember His promise to
Abraham. In doing so, God reminded the people of His faithfulness.
Israel needed to remember God's promises to Abraham. After all, they
were his descendants and thus entitled to partake in God's covenant,
dwelling in the land of promise (see Heb. 11:9). This scene reminds
me that power resides in remembering God's promises.

**Power resides
in remembering
God's promises.**

Look up the following passages and draw a line to match the reference
below to the promise God makes to us.

Spirit anointed

Deuteronomy 31:6   God equips us to do what He calls us to do.

Romans 8:39   God will never leave us. *or forsake*

Isaiah 61:1-3   Nothing can separate us from the love of God.

TAKE ACTION

When we commit to a life of <u>sanctification</u> <u>without compromise</u>, we will inevitably hear God's voice more clearly. If you desire to follow God with your whole heart and life, pray this prayer:

Heavenly Father,
I will remember your call on my life. I will remember your promises and protection. I commit to leave behind things that take my attention away from You.
Like Abraham, I will follow you so that I might pursue your calling on my life. I desire to live a sanctified life—not out of guilt—but out of a grateful heart.
God, thank you for all you've given me. Today, determined to die to the old and live uncompromisingly for you by the Holy Spirit's power, I start anew.
In Jesus name I pray, Amen.

Write today's date here ___3/7/2012_____

DAY 4
Committed to Serve

Yesterday we looked at two reasons Joshua gave explaining why the children of Israel should willingly and uncompromisingly surrender to God. Today, as we discuss the third and fourth reasons for choosing obedience, we will focus more intently on God's commitment to guide us. He is our protector and the source of our life-purpose. Understanding these important truths will better position us to hear His voice.

3. Remember the Protection

As I look back at my life, I can see God's protective hand. To preserve His promises to me, He has had to preserve me, the recipient.

I got my first car when I was a freshmen at the University of Houston. I was so excited by the freedom the car represented that I took three of my friends for a ride. The night was rainy, and as I stopped for a red light, my car began to skid. Wheels screeching, we slid from the center lane into the right, striking the back of another car. I got out to apologize and to survey the damage to my new vehicle. But as I stooped over my car's front end, it suddenly leaped forward.

Like a metal beast, it charged at me. Feeling as if I were trapped in a nightmare, I crashed into the windshield and bounced painfully to the street.

Only later did I realize that another driver had also spun out of control, helpless to prevent the impact that sent me flying. My friends labored to climb out of my car's jammed doors. One of them stooped beside me as another ran for help.

I lay in the street unable to move as the rain continued to pour and my friend spoke words of encouragement. But our adventure was not over.

The slick street claimed yet another car, sending it careening in our direction. Though he frantically honked his horn, the driver could not control his vehicle. With no time to pull me away from the speeding vehicle's path, the people around me ran to the curb as the car twirled wildly in our direction. I lifted my head to see the headlights rushing at me and thought, *my life is over.*

But God had other plans. Amazingly, the driver regained control and his vehicle slid into the roadside bushes. My heart pounding and my eyes wide, I collapsed back onto the road and succumbed to shock. But as I lay there, the Lord spoke through the rain and my mental fog. He protected me from the skidding car. And to this day I believe He instructed His angels to push that car to the side of the road.

DAILY BREAD

"Your fathers cried out to the LORD, so He put darkness between you and the Egyptians, and brought the sea over them, engulfing them. Your own eyes saw what I did to Egypt. After that you lived in the wilderness a long time."
Joshua 24:7

Look up the following verses in your Bible and note below what each says about God's protection.

Deuteronomy 23:14: *Lord moves about in your camp to protect you*

2 Samuel 22:31: *He is a shield for all who take refuge in him.*

Psalm 46:1: *Our refuge our strength ever present help in times of trouble*

Psalm 62:7: *my mighty rock + refuge*

God protects His people. He certainly doesn't protect us from hardship and trouble, but He protects us through them, even to heaven's door. God is a refuge, a stronghold, a defender, and protector. He is a loving God whose greatest desire is to shelter us and protect us from our enemies.

After telling the Israelites about the call and promises of God, Joshua reminded them how God protects and brings to pass His own promises. Consider the progression of Joshua 24:4-12.

- He protected the seed of Abraham so as to preserve the lineage and inheritance of Jacob (v. 4).
- He protected the seed of Jacob even while in the captivity of Pharaoh and delivered them out of his hand (v. 5).

- He continued protecting the children of Israel by dividing the Red Sea when the angry Egyptians pursued them relentlessly. The very waters that were Israel's guard became Egypt's grave (vv. 6-7).
- He gave the Amorites into their hand and allowed them to take possession of their enemy's land (v. 8).
- He turned the curse of Balaam into a blessing and delivered them from Balaam's hand (vv. 9-10).
- He enabled them to safely cross the Jordan and escape from and conquer their enemies at Jericho (v. 11).
- He sent the hornet before the army of Israel into the territory of the Amorites to drive out the kings and conquer them in battle (v. 12).

The list of how God protects His promises goes on and on! God keeps His promises in spite of our sin, our complaints, and the roadblocks we put up. He is faithful to perform that which He has promised.

How has God protected you in order to preserve His calling and promises? Prepare to share your response with your group.

abusive husband - delivered me

restored my soul

4. Remember the Source

Read Joshua 24:12-13. What does God remind the people after showing them the power of His calling, promise, and protection? Check all that apply.

☒ The things they received were not of their own making.
☑ God is in control.
❑ They had to go out and provide for themselves.
❑ The people earned what they got.

God is so good and does so much on our behalf. He is responsible for every good thing that happens to us. Joshua is quick to remind the children of Israel of this fact. God alone is the source of their victory and the fulfillment of His promise. Like the children of Israel, we have no excuse for not completely and totally dedicating our lives to His service.

TAKE ACTION

For what good things do you tend to take credit when the credit belongs to the Father alone?

_____

Take time now to surrender those things back to Him, giving Him all the credit.

In the past two lessons you have studied the incentives Joshua gives for living holy life without compromise. List those four incentives below.

1. _protection_   2. _Blessing_

3. _a great nation_   4. _separation from old self_
                                                sin

After reminding the people of all God had done on their behalf, Joshua challenges the people to make a decision to be set apart to God without compromise. "Choose for yourselves today whom you will serve" (Josh. 24:15, NASB). Having a relationship with God that results in intimate communication begins with a <u>decision</u>. We must immediately and urgently <u>decide</u> to fear the Lord and serve Him in <u>sincerity</u> and truth.

Obedience from the Heart

As a child, I hated Sundays because of kitchen duty. My mother cooked delicious dinners every Sunday afternoon, catering to six family members and inevitable guests. Although such meals were wonderful, I always dreaded them because they required lots of work and clean-up. As I watched her cook, I could only think of the aftermath.

The dishes seemed never ending, and I hated every minute of washing them. I only cleaned them because I was forced to, but I made no effort to hide my distaste with every dish I scrubbed, pot I cleaned, and countertop I wiped.

Today things are different. Sunday dinner is still at Mom's house. And though the meals still make for a lot of work, I no longer dread supper's end. Maybe my feelings have changed because I have my own family now and appreciate how

DAILY BREAD

*The Lord said:
Because these
people approach
Me with their
mouths
to honor Me
with lip service—
yet their hearts
are far from Me,
and their worship
consists of man
made rules
learned [by rote]—
therefore I will
again confound
these people
with wonder
after wonder.
The wisdom of
their wise men
will vanish,
and the
understanding
of the perceptive
will be hidden.
Isaiah 29:13-14*

hard it is to cook a meal and clean up. Maybe it's because I have grown more patient over the years or because my parents no longer force my participation. Whatever the reason, I now willingly offer to take care of the Sunday dishes out of a sincere thankfulness that stems from my heart.

Romans 6 signals a basic change of motivation for believers. We die to our old lives and are reborn in Christ. What can be a stronger motive against sin than the love of Christ?

In verse 17 Paul teaches us another valuable lesson in living sanctified lives: "Thanks be to God that though you were slaves of sin, you became obedient from the heart to that form of teaching to which you were committed" (NASB). Here Paul stresses the core of lifestyle sanctification as a sincere heart passion to obey.

We have all done things "for God" out of religious duty instead of a sincere heart that is eager to obey the Father. Sometimes we do things simply because they are the right thing to do or because we are following tradition. But if our hearts are not behind good deeds, we will miss the blessing and joy available to us through our service. *religious duty vs sincere heart*

Describe in your own words the difference between from-the-heart obedience and ritual obedience.

have to vs choose to

If you desire to build up eternal treasure in heaven, you must choose to follow God with an obedient heart. Matthew 22:37 tells us to, "Love the Lord your God with all your heart, with all your soul, and with all your mind." Only actions built on His love and an honest desire to please Him will do. God is not flattered by formal acts of worship unless they stem from the hearts of people who are genuine in their affection for Him.

List religious activities or good deeds in which you regularly participate. Your list could include anything from going to church, to doing this Bible study, to preparing dinner for your family, to feeding the poor.

Activities/Deeds	+/-	For Whom?
BSF		*dinner Wednesday*
dinners mom/dad		*God*
visit Patti		
This study		
Church		
Chaplain Course		

Put a plus sign beside each activity you can honestly say is done for Christ. Place a minus sign beside those done to impress or please someone else or out of duty and tradition. If you aren't certain why you do something, mark it with a question mark. Carefully consider the activities that have minus signs. In the last column, list for whom you do these activities.

As sanctified believers, our every activity is to bring God glory. Whether we are typing letters, peeling potatoes, or changing dirty diapers, we can honor God in all we do.

> When you face an unpleasant task, how would your attitude change if you saw it as your personal act of worship?

Joy

_____

_____

_____

I'm afraid we often do things for tradition's sake rather than out of our passion for the Lord. I think of a spot on our church's front lawn. Over the years, congregants wore a path. The new trail leaves the sidewalk and cuts though the flowers and between the trees. The path was created by a few people taking a short cut from one building to another, but after a while the path became so obvious that *everyone* started to use it.

> If you were using the story above for a children's sermon, what lesson would you draw from people's behavior?

follow the crowd

_____

_____

When we forget that our entire life is an act of worship, we can begin to take the short cut. After all, everyone's doing it. Let's live differently. Let's practice honoring God in the little things of life. The more nobody notices, the more we can enjoy the private affirmation of the Father. In the process we'll be positioning ourselves at His feet and listening for His voice.

obey me & I will be your God & you my people

TAKE ACTION

What do 1 Samuel 15:22 and Jeremiah 7:23 state as a true desire of God?

Obeying voice of God – better than offerings & sacrifice

Ask the Lord to replace any hypocrisy or ritualism in your life with <u>genuine affection for Him</u>. Tell Him that you desire to obey Him with your whole heart so you may clearly hear His voice. If this isn't yet your desire, tell God honestly and ask Him for the desire to desire Him.

As you end this week think back over the lessons. What changes do you need to implement to be set apart like Samuel when He heard God speak? Complete the following sentences with the specific actions. To be set apart to God, I will seek to:

die daily to *sin – selfish desires*

live to *Christ obedience*

not compromise in *devotion*

serve from passion rather than tradition when *serving*

---

1 J.F. Walvoord and Roy B. Zuck, *The Bible Knowledge Commentary: An Exposition of the Scriptures* (Wheaton: Victor Books, 1998). electronic ed.

good things → too busy

Job 33 -

Viewer Guide
Session 4

Stop working it out

*The lamp of God had not yet gone out, and **Samuel was lying down** in the temple of the LORD where the ark of God was.*

—1 Samuel 3:3

Samuel was __still.__ *(lying down when heard God's voice)*

Jesus said, "Have the people sit down."

—John 6:10

John 6 feeding 5,000

Lord, why?

A special __purpose__

till you build trust

Lord, where?

A special __place__

green grass track record history what he's done

Lord, how?

A special __power__

A Still Attentiveness

MY FATHER WAS A LIFEGUARD DURING COLLEGE. Growing up, he told me many stories about the lives he was privileged to save. On one occasion he saw a struggling man and quickly swam out to meet him. However, he couldn't do anything to help because the victim was so afraid that he was frantically waving and kicking in an effort to save himself. My father kept calling out to the man to be still so he could do what he was trained to do but the fearful young man couldn't hear him. My father had no other choice but to wait. He treaded water nearby until the drowning man got too tired to fight for his own life. As soon as he got tired, gave up, and became still my father swam in and did what he intended to do all along: save one who might otherwise be lost.

God desires to speak to us but often we are too busy to hear Him. Our frantic attempts to fix our own problems keep us from hearing His calming voice, receiving His instructions, and allowing him to do what He intended to do all along: save one who might otherwise be lost.

DAY 1
Still in My Mind

I know a young woman who struggled with an eating disorder for more than a decade. She said that she knew Satan used her mind to keep her in bondage by continually filling it with destructive thoughts from fear of gaining weight to low self-esteem. The enemy used these as a tool to keep her from recognizing God's love and acceptance and to keep her from hearing His voice.

Our minds are battlefields, not theme parks! This truth becomes apparent when we can't sleep, eat, or think straight because of the tug-of-war within our heads. Two forces are "raised up" against our ability to clearly hear God's voice. Today we'll look at a strategy for winning the spiritual war for our minds.

Look closely at 2 Corinthians 10:5 in the margin on page 67.
What two forces oppose the knowledge of God?
❏ obedience to Christ   ❏ speculations
❏ lofty things   ❏ every thought

Our minds are one of the hardest areas for us to control, yet they are often the easiest for Satan to use against us. From lustful thoughts to regretful ones, guilty reminders of the past to vengeful imaginations, our minds fill with images that can pull us away from the Lord, His voice, and His plan for our lives.

We must consider three questions as we prepare to fight the battle for our minds. Who is our enemy? What are our weapons? What is our battle strategy?

The True Enemy

To ensure victory in any battle, we must first identify the enemy; otherwise, our battle plan will be misdirected.

According to 1 Peter 5:8 who is our adversary? _____

Fighting tirelessly against negative thoughts is futile; thoughts have no power on their own. Instead, we must concern ourselves with the true enemy of our souls. When we listen to God's voice, the devil fears us. He will do anything to hinder us from hearing from God. He actively roams the earth seeking whom he may destroy (see Job 2:2), and he wants to use our minds as tools to destroy us.

Looking at Satan's role in my thought life helps me gain a new perspective. When I recognize the enemy as I struggle with lustful, fearful, or guilty thoughts, I get angry! That righteous anger energizes me. God intends for us to get mad when the devil pursues our minds by infiltrating our thoughts. When we recognize our true enemy we know where to direct our spiritual weaponry.

The Weapons

We find the key to combatting the devil's pursuit of our minds in 2 Corinthians. Paul gives key information regarding how we can win the war.

Read 2 Corinthians 10:3-4. What do spiritual weapons demolish?
❑ buildings   ❑ governments   ❑ fortresses   ❑ armies

Our enemy is a spiritual being who fights a *spiritual* war against us. Satan's goal and desire is to fill our minds with arguments and strongholds that will keep us from a close relationship with God.

Which of the following examples of Satanic argument has he used on you lately?
❑ Disobedience doesn't really have serious consequences (see Gen. 3:4).
❑ You can do better if you will be your own boss (see Gen. 3:5).
❑ You should be free to worship as you choose (see Matt. 4:8-10).
❑ You are not valuable to God or anyone else (see Matt. 10:30-31).
❑ Your sins are too numerous for God to forgive (see Isa.44:21-22).

For though we walk in the flesh, we do not war according to the flesh, for the weapons of our warfare are not of the flesh, but divinely powerful for the destruction of fortresses.
2 Cor. 10:3-4, NASB

Paul understood that his business was to "demolish arguments and every high-minded thing that is raised up against the knowledge of God" (2 Cor. 10:4-5). He fought a battle for the believers' minds. And he knew that fleshly weapons could not help. Paul realized human wisdom would not tear down the barriers and strongholds in the minds of the people to whom he preached. He also knew barriers and strongholds would keep people from hearing God's voice.

The Battle Strategy

Remember the woman with the eating disorder? I asked how she won the war of her mind. She told me she purposely filled her mind with the Word of God to combat the enemy of her soul. We need weapons of divine power to fight the supernatural battle of the mind. Seminars, counseling, and discussions are wonderful tools, but alone they are not adequate weapons to fight a spiritual war. In Ephesians 6 Paul lists the weapons to win the war. For the sake of time, I'll focus on only a few of the items Paul mentions. First, consider the shield of faith.

A Roman soldier's shield was made of wood but overlaid with linen and leather. This design enabled it to absorb an enemy's fiery arrows. The shield provided protection for the soldier's entire body. Heavy and cumbersome, the shields caused them discomfort but often proved necessary to save their lives.

Like those shields, faith in Christ can cause discomfort. In a world that does not believe in the validity of God or His Word, faith will often demand uncomfortable choices.

How does our faith function like the Roman soldier's shield?

_____

Spiritual safety comes through faith. Let the faith you have in Christ remind you of the great inheritance you have in Christ and serve as a guard of protection on your mind. Use it to protect your thoughts against the enemy's advances.

One of the last pieces of equipment a Roman soldier put on was his helmet. Having his head covered gave a soldier safety that helped him move boldly forward in battle. It encouraged him to fight with confidence.

How can putting on the "helmet of salvation" cause you to walk more confidently?

_____

The Word of God is the sword of the Spirit (see Eph. 6:17). Second Timothy 3:16-17 says, "All Scripture is inspired by God and is profitable for teaching, for rebuking, for correcting, for training in righteousness, so that the man of God may be complete, equipped for every good work."

How does Psalm 19:7 describe the Lord's instruction? (Check all that apply.)

❑ complicated   ❑ trustworthy   ❑ confusing

❑ perfect   ❑ available to all   ❑ wise

When the Holy Spirit supernaturally applies the Word of God to your life you can begin to gain control over your thought life. To know and understand the Scriptures is to know and understand God's power (see Mark 12:24).

When I purposefully fill my mind with the Word of God, particularly before retiring for the night, my thoughts focus not on my day but on what I read. The very power of God through the living words of Scripture combats the strongholds that take up residence in my mind.

Think of the sword of the Spirit as your "dagger." Every time you feel your mind is running away with inappropriate thoughts or imaginations, quickly jab those thoughts with the Word.

The instruction of the LORD is perfect, reviving the soul; the testimony of the LORD is trustworthy, making the inexperienced wise.

Psalm 19:7

Read Matthew 4:1-11. Three times Jesus uses Scripture as a dagger against Satan's attempts to manipulate Him. In the margin, describe Jesus' answers in your own words.

Briefly describe one negative thought with which you struggle. Then search Scripture to find a "dagger" to use against that thought. Consider using a concordance, a topical Bible, or Bible software.

My struggle: _____

My dagger: _____

*Keep a blank piece of paper in your Bible labeled "My Dagger List." When you come across Scriptures you can use in the war for your mind, write them down and save for future use. God's Word is the only thing that can annihilate the ungodly thoughts that plague our minds.

Search the following passages to learn how to respond to these specific negative thoughts. Fill in the chart with your findings.

Negative Thought	Scripture Reference	Truth
I am inadequate.	1 Peter 1:3	
I've messed up too much in my past.	Philippians 3:13	
I will never be free from this sin.	John 8:36	
I am insignificant.	Jeremiah 1:5	
I am a mistake.	Psalm 139:14	

Ask the Lord to help you to control runaway thoughts. Tell Him that you desire to hear His voice clearly. Request that He help you actively shield yourself against the fiery darts of the enemy so you can be still in your mind.

TAKE ACTION

Getting our minds under control is not a battle we can win once and for all. We have to remain alert. Luke 4:13 tells us that after the wilderness temptation of Jesus "the devil departed from Him for a time." Satan seeks ways to re-enter the war zone of our minds to ensure his own victory. In being alert to the enemy's future attacks, Paul suggests that we fill our minds with six things.

Look up Philippians 4:8 in your Bible. List Paul's suggestions.
1.
2.
3.
4.
5.
6.

Dwell on the validity of Scripture to combat the dishonest and unreliable messages you will receive from the world in which we live. God wants to speak to us. We must keep our minds free of anything that will stand in the way.

DAY 2
Still in My Confidence

My sister Chrystal and I used to play "the trust game." She stood behind me, and I would close my eyes and fall back into her arms. On one occasion she allowed me to fall back into her arms five or six times without incident. Each time as she caught me, she built up my confidence in her. However, on the seventh time, she let me down—literally. She stepped away, and I went crashing to the floor. The betrayal of trust hurt much worse than the landing.

The Lord continually asks us to keep falling back into His waiting arms. The very foundation of Christianity is our faith in Christ's ability to forgive our sins through the sacrifice of His life and the victory of His resurrection. Today we will look at the concept of confidence, exploring its role in our ongoing relationship with Christ.

Read Ruth 1:5-22. According to the last line of verse 16, in whom did

Ruth place her confidence? _____

DAILY BREAD
*Jesus replied,
"The healthy don't
need a doctor,
but the sick do."*
Luke 5:31

Ruth trusted Naomi, but she ultimately placed her trust in Naomi's God. Ruth set an example for us to follow. As Ruth placed her confidence in Naomi's God, we place our confidence in God through Jesus. In Ruth 3, Boaz, Ruth's employer, commends her not only for her initial confidence in God but her ongoing faith despite her circumstances.

What circumstances in Ruth 2:11-12 does Boaz mention that could have caused Ruth's confidence in God to waver?

_____

What circumstances in your life cause your faith to waver?

_____

Have you sought refuge in God for those situations? ❑ yes ❑ no How?

_____

_____

Just as salvation can only come when we truly transfer our confidence from ourselves to Jesus, our ability to live victorious Christian lives comes only as we place that same confidence in Christ daily. Whether in business or personal matters we usually find assurance when we are self-reliant and trust in our own abilities. It's so easy for us to trust in ourselves, but it is difficult for most of us to admit our faults, face our weakness, and ask God for the help we need.

We must recognize our limitations, because only Christ can take care of our problems. We must place our confidence in Him alone. In Luke 5:31 Jesus clearly states that He came for those who are sick and in need of help. Jesus likens Himself to a physician. Like any good doctor, He's available to people who are aware they are sick, admit they are sick, and come to Him with confidence.

Think of the last time you visited a physician. What was wrong? What was the deciding factor that made you choose to see a physician?

_____

_____

My husband is not quick to go to a doctor's office. He will sit at home with a sore throat and a fever for days before calling to make an appointment with the doctor. In the meantime he hopes for relief, filling himself with juice and over-the-counter medications. I feel so sorry for him as he cuddles up in the bed, shivering from fever and sniffling with a cold. Each time I wonder how long he will suffer before admitting how sick he is.

We often treat spiritual sickness like Jerry with physical illness. We either don't realize we are spiritually sick or don't realize the extent of it. We may think we simply lack interest in church when we really have spiritual cancers like greed and bitterness. Until someone points out our condition, we may not realize how bad off we are. Often others can see more then we can.

Consider the last time you had company. Maybe you knew you needed to clean the living room before they arrived but never got around to it. When the visitors stepped into your home, you suddenly became conscious of the dust bunny under the sofa and the coffee stain on the end table. In the same way, when we bring another believer into our spiritual living rooms, we suddenly become aware of the broken areas of our lives.

15This saying is trustworthy and deserving of full acceptance: "Christ Jesus came into the world to save sinners"—and I am the worst of them. 16But I received mercy because of this, so that in me, the worst [of them], Christ Jesus might demonstrate the utmost patience as an example to those who would believe in Him for eternal life.
1 Timothy 1:15-16

Call a close friend and ask her to "come into your spiritual living room." Ask her to point out the areas of your life in need of the Physician's touch. Make a list of her comments in the margin.

Awareness does not equal admitting. I might be aware that my living room is dirty yet still not admit I need to do something about it.

Read 1 Timothy 1:15-16 and answer the following.

What did Jesus come to do (v. 15)?

_____

What does Paul admit about himself (v. 15)?

_____

_____

What did Paul find as a result of this (v. 16)?

_____

We must abandon the confidence we have in our own ability to fix our problems. God can turn our circumstances around when we admit our needs and place our confidence in Him alone.

Read the following examples of those who realized their limitations and admitted their needs to God. Note what happened in each case as a result.

Example	Result
2 Chronicles 20:2-3,22	
Isaiah 1:16-18	
Mark 10:47-52	
Luke 4:40	
Luke 8:43-48	
Luke 12:5-12	

When my husband finally calls the doctor, he is so glad he did and wonders why he waited so long. Likewise, when you and I finally admit our need, call on Jesus, and place our confidence in Him, we often wonder why we held onto our suffering when we had the answer for our struggles all along.

The reason doctors get medical degrees is to help us when we are ill. It makes sense to go to the expert with physical illness. Jesus said the reason He came was to be a physician to those who are sick. So why are we so reluctant to admit our need and go to the Great Physician?

In Luke 5 Jesus sat with tax collectors and sinners. The community ostracized these people because of their occupations. Tax collectors often used their status to steal from the people, so tax collectors were constantly looked upon with disdain. They could not escape awareness of their sickness; it came with the job. But these particular tax collectors and sinners did something in response to their need; they went to dinner with Jesus.

These tax collectors took a step of faith. They visited the Great Physician. This step of going to the "doctor" is so important—not just for those who are saved but also for those who do not yet know Him.

John 3:16 clearly states that God sent His Son to die for those who needed saving but that salvation only comes to those who "believe on Him." Our walk with Christ began when we removed the confidence we had in our ability to save ourselves and decided to trust Him instead. Our ability to live victoriously while here on earth depends on our willingness to put our confidence in Him.

After admitting our need to the doctor and placing confidence in Him, we must daily follow the doctor's recipe for recovery. My husband may admit he is sick, call to make an appointment, and even drive to the doctor's office, but those actions won't heal him. If the doctor orders a prescription, Jerry must get it filled and faithfully take the medicine. If the doctor gives instructions, he must follow them. The level of confidence Jerry has in the doctor's ability shows up in how faithfully he sticks to the physician's instructions.

The dinner in Luke 5 was in Jesus' honor. The banquet was in the home of a tax collector named Levi who would later be called Matthew. In response to Jesus' command to follow Him, he invited Jesus into His home for a celebration and reception.

Jesus' "prescription" to Levi in verse 27 is the same as His instruction to us.

Write it. _____

Levi left behind his family, career, money, friends, home, security, and much more because he believed Christ had more to offer. So confident was he in this decision that he threw a party to celebrate!

Why would a man find cause for celebration in "leaving everything behind" (v. 28)?

_____

I think the account points to a basic misconception. We don't really give up anything to follow Christ. Instead, we make a wise value judgment. Levi believed the man for whom he left everything was more valuable than what he gave up. In the words of Jim Elliot: "He is no fool who gives what he cannot keep to gain what he cannot lose."[1]

TAKE ACTION

What things might you have to leave behind to fully trust in Christ?

_____

_____

What emotions accompany your decision to leave these things behind?

_____

If you struggle with matters that disrupt your peace, apply Psalm 46:10 to them. Be still and know that He is God.

DAY 3
Still in My Emotions

Jenny has every right to be an emotional basket case, but her smile shows the security and peace she finds in the Lord. Nothing in Jenny's life seems easy. She has had 50 operations to try to cure a muscular disease that puzzles her doctors. She has never known a day without extreme pain. Jenny's father was killed by a doctor's error. Her mother will have 8 operations over the next few years to deal with her own medical problems. Despite all of this Jenny says, "I thank God for every single thing I have lived through."

Ruth must have been somewhat like my friend Jenny. Not only had Ruth lost her husband, but she relocated to a new place where she likely did not know the language or the social customs. Her life was not easy. Such hardships and difficulties could have emotionally destroyed her.

With the situations Ruth and Jenny faced, many of us would lock ourselves in our bedrooms! Tough circumstances can easily get the best of us emotionally. Yet Scripture shows Ruth dealing with her circumstances extremely well. She expressed her emotions (see Ruth 1:9,14), but we don't see her overcome by them. How did Old Testament Ruth and modern America Jenny rest so assuredly in the arms of God while in such personal pain?

DAILY BREAD

Moses said to the people: "Don't be afraid. Stand firm and see the LORD's salvation He will provide for you today … The Lord will fight for you; you must be quiet."
Exodus 14:13-14

What hardship are you facing right now in your life?

_____

Contrast the emotional reactions of the people in the following Scriptures with Ruth's reaction to her circumstances.

Hannah—1 Samuel 1:6-7 _____

Jonah—Jonah 4:1-3 _____

King Ahab—1 Kings 21:4 _____

Which character's actions best describe your reaction to personal difficulty?
❑ Ruth   ❑ Hannah   ❑ Jonah   ❑ King Ahab

Runaway Feelings

You are certainly not alone if hard times make you weep or grow angry. Emotions are not wrong. Scripture doesn't say that we are not to feel. In fact, God Himself exhibits many emotions ranging from joy (see Zeph. 3:17) to anger (see 2 Kings 21:6). We know that Jesus was sinless (see 2 Cor. 5:21), but even

He experienced anger (see Mark 3:5) and a sadness that caused Him to weep (see John 11:35). The problem is that many of us allow our feelings to dictate our actions and affect our decisions. Worse, we sometimes let our emotions justify inappropriate actions. Runaway emotions can block out God's voice and keep us from following God's road map for our lives.

About a year ago, a friend asked me to provide the biblical foundation for a how-to book she was writing. Immediately, excitement overtook me. Thrilled that she had approached me, I told her right away that I would work with her on the project, and we began to move forward.

About two months into the process, I began to feel uneasy about my participation. The Holy Spirit began to convict me about my hurried decision to move ahead without first consulting Him. He showed me that my enthusiasm had caused me to say "yes" to a project that He hadn't planned for me to participate in at that time.

After a few days of stalling, I had to call my friend and back out of the project. I was so embarrassed and upset to disappoint her. Although she made it easy on me, I still wish that I hadn't let my emotions talk me into doing something that was clearly not part of God's plan for me.

Emotions are fickle and change at a moment's notice. (Most of us can go from crying one moment to laughing the next during a good movie!) Feelings should never be the final decision maker in our lives.

What emotions do you struggle to keep under control?

_____

_____

Emotions do serve us in another way; they provide a window into our minds and hearts. They reveal what we believe. For example, when Jackson was three months old, we moved him from the bassinet in our room to his upstairs nursery. How far away that nursery seemed during that first month of separation! I couldn't sleep. I was wide awake with fear.

My imagination created potential scenarios in which my baby was somehow hurt. My fears extended to horrible, impractical occurrences. I was sure his room would cave in and he would fall to his death. A kidnapper might climb through Jackson's second story window. A tornado might rip the roof off the nursery. A rabid dog might get inside our home. Fear consumed me.

Finally remembering that God is always in full control, I had a decision to make. Would I allow fear to control my actions by stealing my sleep or even causing me to sleep in my child's room? Or would I let go of my fears, giving them to God? My display of fear exposed to me the gap between what I said I believed and what I really felt.

The Snowball Effect

Ephesians 4:26-27 clearly warns that allowing our emotions to gain control of our actions gives Satan an avenue and opportunity to work in our lives. When he gets to our emotions, the snowball effect begins and they become bigger and dirtier as we allow them to roll.

Be angry and do not sin. Don't let the sun go down on your anger, and don't give the Devil an opportunity.
Ephesians 4:26-27

Choose two of the following emotions you have experienced and describe how the snowball effect can cause them to grow:

Worry	Anger	Grief	Loneliness
Shame	Frustration	Resentment	Depression

1. _____

2. _____

In Exodus 14:13-14 Moses told the people not to be afraid. Rewrite this passage in the margin, substituting the emotions that seek to control you.

Banking on God's Promises

Remembering God's promises helps us greatly in the task of controlling our emotions. Moses didn't just tell the Israelites to stop being afraid, he also gave them a reason they could. He said, "the Lord will fight for you." That information gave them reason to relinquish their fears.

Read the following verses. After God tells these individuals not to fear, He follows with words of encouragement. Summarize those encouragements.

Genesis 15:1_____

Deuteronomy 31:6_____

1 Chronicles 28:20_____

Isaiah 41:13 _____

God's promises can act as the catalyst we need to relinquish any consuming emotions. Are you lonely? The Lord says, "I am with you always" (Matt. 28:20). Are you afraid? The Lord says, "My peace I give to you" (John 14:27). Are you anxious or worried? The Lord says, "Though the mountains move and the hills shake, My love will not be removed from you" (Isa. 54:10). Are you angry and seeking revenge? The Lord says, "Vengeance is mine. I will repay" (Rom. 12:19).

Experiencing emotion is not wrong; letting emotions consume and control us is. Let God's promises show you how to think and act.

TAKE ACTION

Be honest with God about your feelings. Instead of allowing your emotions to steer you away from God, purposefully turn your attention to the Lord in times of intense emotional stress. Tell Him your struggles and ask Him to reveal His perspective and power.

Talk to the Lord about any all-consuming emotions you are experiencing. Ask Him to help you be emotionally still so your actions can be controlled by what you know to be true rather than by what you feel.

Write your prayer.

_____

_____

_____

DAY 4
Still in My Ambitions

DAILY BREAD

Be still, and know that I am God: I will be exalted among the nations, I will be exalted in the earth.
Psalm 46:10, ASV

Too often we don't hear the voice of God because we don't want to. We fear God might ask us to do something that goes against our plans.

Before I understood God's calling on my life, I wanted to be a Christian singer. I prepared by singing at every opportunity. I rehearsed constantly. I spoke with successful Christian artists, seeking advice on what steps to take and when to take them. I surrounded myself with music and key people in the industry, but time passed and I saw no results.

Discouraged, I became anxious and worried. Door after door closed in my face. Yet instead of accepting them as signals that God wanted me to move in a different direction, I allowed my ambition to turn into selfishness. I began to disregard God's leading, trying to kick the doors of the music industry down on my own. The desire to sing controlled me. I made phone calls, sent tapes, and tried to create singing opportunities, but God had other plans for me.

All that time I spent trying so hard to make things happen, I was fighting against God's will. How grateful I am that He allowed me to discover His plan in spite of my foolishness.

Have you had a similar experience, where you could not turn loose of your desires? ❑ yes ❑ no   If so, describe the situation in the margin.

I used to proudly define myself as an ambitious person. Then the Lord revealed to me the sinful nature of ambition apart from His leadership. We must allow nothing to control our actions and drown out the sound of God's voice.

Which of the following best describes your ambitions or desires?
❑ making more money   ❑ having children
❑ getting married   ❑ getting promoted
❑ maintaining a youthful appearance   ❑ taking a dream vacation
❑ starting a ministry   ❑ getting my college degree

Problems with Ambition

Ambition implies a desire and willingness to do whatever it takes to reach a goal for the purpose of achieving earthly status, notoriety, or power. Ambitious people are in danger of being controlled by ambition rather than the voice of God.

Look up the following examples of individuals whose ambition got them into trouble. Record God's response beside each example.

Example	God's response
Lucifer—Isaiah 14:12-15	
Adam and Eve—Genesis 3:5-6,14-16	
Tower of Babel—Genesis 11:4,8-9	
Adonijah—1 Kings 1:5; 1 Kings 2:24	

Our ambitions often reveal a deeper desire for status, fame, or power. Most of what we strive for and desire finds its root in one of those three areas. Paul calls these desires "confidence in the flesh" (Phil. 3:3-4). Worldly ambition is a desire to find fulfillment in the things that please us instead of pleasing God.

Describe how the following Scriptures speak to the issue of our ambition.

Ecclesiastes 2:11_____

Matthew 6:26-34 _____

John 14:27 _____

TAKE ACTION

God gives us the freedom to prepare, plan, and position ourselves to achieve our goals. Proverbs 16:3 applauds people who plan wisely to reach their goals. Ultimately, however, we must "be still" in our ambitions and relax in the knowledge that God is sovereign and His design and purposes for our lives are better than our own. We must not allow ambition to control our actions.

How might ambition hurt your ability to hear from God?

_____

Have you crossed the line from Godly planning to selfish ambition in a particular area of your life? ❏ yes ❏ no   If so, how?

_____

Ask the Lord to show you what steps you should take to submit to His will for you. Tell Him that you desire His plans more then your own and you are willing to exchange your selfish ambition for His agenda for your life. Can you accept God's instructions to be still and know that He is God?

DAY 5
Still in My Actions

Sometimes it seems infinitely harder to find the time to sit still before Him than it is to cook dinner, read, or even clean the house. Life seems to press in on my quiet time, pulling my attention away from God.

Which of the following activities is the most difficult for you to make time to do? (Underline your answer.)

cook dinner   read a book   clean the house
talk on the phone   surf the Internet   meditate and pray

The simple instruction to "be still" permeates Scripture. In Isaiah 30 God speaks to obstinate Israelites determined to go about their plans without regard for His.

In the midst of their busyness, God offers them salvation from their enemies and peace in the midst of their problems.

What was Israel trying to do that was not pleasing to God (Isa. 30:1-2)?

_____

The nation of Israel faced a problem. Enemies threatened their security. The Israelites did everything in their power to try to solve the problem through human measures. Unfortunately, nothing they did seemed to work. In the midst of all of their efforts God said, "In quietness and rest is your strength." The futility of our efforts may be the voice of God calling us to be still in Him instead of trying to work things out on our own.

What is a current situation you're trying to figure out yourself that you need to take before the Lord? Describe the situation in the margin.

Their history could have taught the Israelites what to do in their time of need. When an army was approaching, King Jehoshaphat called a national fast and sought the Lord. You can read King Jehoshaphat's prayer in 2 Chronicles 20:6-12. Instead of frantically seeking his own solution, He simply looked to God.

Paraphrase God's response to Jehoshaphat's prayer in 2 Chronicles 20:17.

_____

I like how *The Message* translates this verse: "You won't have to lift a hand in this battle; just stand firm, Judah and Jerusalem, and watch God's saving work for you take shape." The devil knows we can find real peace and freedom in our lives when we turn to God and trust Him. This is why Satan desires nothing more than to keep us busy.

Do you handle trouble more like the children of Israel in:
❏ Isaiah's day or ❏ Jehoshaphat's day?

According to 1 Samuel 3:3-4 what was Samuel doing in the temple when the Lord spoke to Him?

_____

How often do you, like Samuel, purposefully spend time in stillness?
❏ at the start of every day   ❏ regularly
❏ occasionally   ❏ you're kidding, right?

The challenge of stillness does not call us to a passive life that requires no effort on our part. The decision to consciously submit to repentance, rest, quiet, and trust is a conscious commitment that requires courage and diligence.

Our job in the battle is to station ourselves. We must fill our place in the line of battle. Sometimes the most difficult response you can make to a challenge is to sit quietly before the Lord. We often want to take on a more aggressive role in fighting personal battles, not realizing that our strength often comes from sitting still.

How can you alter your schedule to make time to be still before God?

_____

By prioritizing and cutting back some useless activities, we could create a wealth of time to dedicate to listening for God's voice.

TAKE ACTION

We need to make listening for God's direction a priority in our daily schedules. Use the space below to list the practical steps you will take to "be still."

To have a daily quiet time, I will _____

_____

To remind myself to pray throughout the day I will _____

_____

To quiet myself when worries overtake me I will _____

_____

To practice trusting the Father more I will_____

_____

1 "Papers of Philip James Elliot—Collection 277," Billy Graham Center archives [online], [cited 19 January 2005]. Available from the Internet *http://www.wheaton.edu/bgc/archives/faq/20.htm.*

Viewer Guide

Session 5

The lamp of God had not yet gone out, and Samuel was lying down **in the temple of the LORD where the ark of God was.**

—1 Samuel 3:3

Samuel got as close as he could to the _____ _____ of God.

As [Jesus] was approaching Jericho, a certain blind man was sitting by the road, begging. Now hearing a crowd going by, he began to inquire what this might be. They told him that Jesus of Nazareth was passing by.

—Luke 18:35-37

1. The manifest presence of God is _____ to you.

2. The manifest presence of God is _____ for you.

Blessed are you who hunger now, for you shall be satisfied.

—Luke 6:21

Ask your friends what you're _____ for.

Ask yourself, *What keeps me awake at night?*

3. The manifest presence of God is _____ to us.

His presence alone is life giving.

A Sold-Out Hunger

I DON'T KNOW HIS NAME but I know his story. He was replacing some counter-tops in our kitchen. He saw my Bible and the floodgates of conversation opened.

"Before I met Christ," he explained, "I was addicted to sex, drugs, and alcohol. I constantly debated leaving my family in search of something to fill my gnawing hunger. The quest left me empty but I kept looking. Until the day God showed up."

One morning an extreme hangover left him trying to recall the night's events. Something inside Him snapped. Tears flowed and a verse his wife had quoted many times came to his mind: "Call to Me, and I will answer you, and I will tell you great and mighty things, which you do not know" (Jer. 33:3). He called out: "God, if You are there and can hear me; I'm desperate." Jesus met him. For the first time in his life the void in His heart was filled. He never had another drink, never touched another drug, and has been faithful to his wife and children since that day.

God meets with those who seek Him with passion. May we hunger for the life-changing presence and voice of God so that we too can encounter His power to change us forever.

DAY 1
Hungry for His Direction

I hesitated to accept Jerry's proposal until I knew the Lord was giving us the green light. I was desperate for His direction. I prayed, "God, I believe You are telling me to move forward with accepting Jerry's offer. I need clarification that Jerry is Your choice for me. I need to hear Your voice."

When God gave Moses instructions to lead the Israelites into the promised land, Moses experienced similar feelings. He wanted specific details on how to proceed, so he prayed earnestly for clarification of directions he had already received.

I love how *The Message* paraphrases Moses' prayer in Exodus 33:12-13: "Look, you tell me, 'Lead this people,' but you don't let me know whom you're going to send with me. You tell me, 'I know you well and you are special to me.' If I am so special to you, let me in on your plans. That way, I will continue being special to you. Don't forget, this is your people, your responsibility."

Moses longed for the Lord's continued direction. He was hungry for it. Moses desired to receive clear guidance regarding *God's* purposes. He earnestly wanted to follow God's plan instead of his own.

Which of the following best describes how you seek God's direction?
❑ I desire God's direction in understanding His purposes for me.
❑ I seek God's blessing on the direction I choose to take.
❑ Sometimes I follow Him; sometimes I follow me.

I've often claimed to desire God's direction for my life while really wanting Him to bless what I want! But God desires that we eagerly and hungrily seek His true plan for us, humbly following in the direction He leads. Sometimes, however, His plans seem difficult to accept.

Your Interruption: God's Intervention

Each day I ask the Lord to guide me. I yield to Him, letting Him know that I desire to be used for His purposes. Unfortunately, however, I often become frustrated when God changes my plans to coincide with His.

I find distractions particularly irritating when I am focused on getting an item crossed off my to-do list. I don't want anyone or anything getting in the way of my schedule. More and more the Lord is showing me what I consider interruptions are often divine distractions designed to reveal His plans for me.

As I write, Jackson tugs on my pants leg, calling "Mommy!" and trying desperately to get my attention. My first inclination is to shoo him away and get back to work, but the Holy Spirit reminds me that Jackson is not an interruption. He is my first ministry! Ignoring this "interruption" ignores God's attempt to move me away from my plan for my day to His.

In truth, we all become frustrated when seemingly meaningless interruptions interfere with plans we have for our careers, families, finances, or ministries. Are we missing God's intervention as He seeks to divert us to His will?

Think of a time when God interrupted you, redirecting your plans to His. How did you respond? Plan to share your story with your group.

_____

Sometimes when our plans are interrupted, we are staring God's direction in the face. We must not push them aside to complete what we feel is most important.

What does Isaiah 55:8-9 reveal about the differences between our plans and the Lord's plans?

_____

DAILY BREAD

He, your Teacher will no longer hide Himself, but your eyes will behold your Teacher. Your ears will hear a word behind you, "This is the way, walk in it, whenever you turn to the right or to the left." Isaiah 30:20-21, NASB

When I read this passage, I'm reminded of all the times life's busyness has blinded me to what God had for me. God sees the big picture. He is in control.

Before I met Jerry, I dated a couple of guys seriously. Each relationship lasted for an extended period of time, so I considered these young men as potential husbands. However, in those days my plans for becoming a wife were repeatedly "interrupted," leaving me frustrated and emotional.

God sees the big picture. He is in control.

Later, when I met Jerry and we cautiously approached the idea of marriage together, I was timid and afraid. I wondered if he were truly "the one." Was getting married the right thing to do?

Hoping for answers, I prayed, searched Scripture, and sought the wise counsel of the minister who had officiated my parents' wedding ceremony. After listening to my concerns, he said something that changed my perspective: "Priscilla, God interrupted your plans on other occasions. If He used those interruptions to guide you to His will, He can and will interrupt anything that goes against His plans for you now. Your job is to be hungry enough to receive His direction. He will reveal it to you." What a freeing thought for me! Relieved, I rejoiced in the life interruptions that had led me to Jerry and found renewed trust in God's guidance.

My minister/counselor was not saying I could pursue any crazy course that came to mind and expect God to interrupt. He knew I had answered the important relationship questions of Christian values and character. I just needed to be sure I was following God's will (see Jas. 4:13-15).

After each of the following case studies, explain the lesson it teaches.

Sarah is a single woman who desires to marry a certain man. While he lacks qualities God admires such as discipline and self-control, he has attributes Sarah prefers such as height, a great career, and fashion sense. Over the last month, Sarah has devoted her attention to this man while ignoring a godly man who is showing interest in her. She sees this second man as an interruption. Because he does not meet all her superficial standards, she misses the fact that he is potentially God's intervention.

Lesson: _____

Claudia is a happily married mother of four who never desired a large family. She always considered herself too career-oriented and free-spirited to be tied down. However, despite efforts to prevent pregnancy, she finds herself carrying a fifth child. She resents this new interruption; her disappointment is clear to her entire family. Claudia doesn't realize that this new baby may be God's divine intervention.

Lesson: _____

Tamara is climbing the corporate ladder. She has worked hard to secure her position in a male-dominated environment, and it seems to be paying off. But one morning she finds that a dip in the economy has made it necessary for her employer to cut staff. She is laid off. Unemployed for the past six months, Tamara has been offered a local ministry position, but the pay is nowhere close to what she's used to and the job's duties seem beneath her degree and experience. Tamara is frustrated, seeing this job as an interruption to her plan for success. She doesn't acknowledge that this could be God's potential intervention.

Lesson: _____

My sister, to continue with your plans without regarding life's interruptions is to ignore God's leading and voice. When you and I desire God's best for us but become annoyed when He steps in to change the course of our lives, we rebel against the very thing we prayed for. Rebellion is a rejection of God and His will for our lives. It can cause us to miss out on the abundant life He offers.

When I graduated college with a degree in communications, I wanted to work in television. Though I tried to get into the business, my phone calls weren't returned, my resumes were not reviewed, and my attempts fell flat. Even a few television shows that I was hired to work on were cancelled shortly after I arrived. All of these problems were major interruptions in my plans. Instead of seeing them as God's divine intervention to reveal His direction for me, I rebelliously kept trying to forge my own path.

Describe an occasion when you executed a plan that was not from God.

_____

What indicators or interruptions were placed in your path to show you that your plans weren't His?

_____

Think about the Israelites, trudging across the desert, grumbling and complaining as they traveled (Isa. 30:6). They brought immense suffering on their heads because they trusted their own wisdom instead of God's. They would not have gone through much of what they did had they aligned themselves with Him.

Why are we so willing to pay the often high price of doing our own thing, when following God's advice is far less expensive and energy consuming? Like the Jews, we are often willing to give away valuables, to travel through dangers, and to experience hardship simply because we want to follow our own direction instead of consulting God. Can you commit to trusting in God's direction even when it seems contrary to what you think you need?

List areas of your life where you need to fervently and completely seek God's guidance.

_____

_____

Scripture says the "Lord longs to be gracious to you ... He waits on high to have compassion on you" (Isa. 30:18, NASB). That message applies to us! God will listen and respond when we go to Him for guidance. God freely gives wisdom to those who ask for it (see Jas. 1:5). When we do, we "will hear a word behind us saying, 'This is the way, walk in it' " (Isa. 30:21, NASB).

DAY 2
Hungry for His Word

"I've heard from God," he says, claiming he received divine instructions to move forward with his plans. With confidence he insists God approves his decisions.

"He" is an outspoken homosexual up for election as a bishop in the Episcopal church. On a nationally broadcast TV show with an audience of thousands, this man insists that God approves his homosexual lifestyle and endorses his position as a church leader.

I sit in stunned shock as I watch—horrified by the declaration that God has supposedly given both his lifestyle and plans for church office the thumbs-up. I listen as the man explains that he has the ability to judge between the voice in his own head, which could very well be his ego, and God's voice. "My decision," he says of his plan to become a bishop, "is certainly one based on the voice of God."

What does Romans 1:24-27 suggest about whether this man heard God correctly on this matter?

_____

Most of us seek God when trying to answer life questions like: "What job should I choose?" "Should I go back to school?" "What neighborhood should we move into?" "Should we go to this church or that one?"

As we seek God's direction and listen for His reply, we must wisely verify that the voice of response is God's and not our own. But how can we make sure that our own voice—our desires and wants—isn't drowning out God's? Before we can answer that, we have to address the fact that everyone seems to claim, "I've heard from God." A man insists God told him to leave his wife and children. Supposedly, the same God who spoke to Moses instructs physicians to end the lives of unborn children and elderly adults. Obviously, God did not really say those things.

We must learn to reconcile what people claim to "hear" God say with the truth of what God really says. Just as important, we must investigate how we can apply that knowledge to our relationship with the Lord.

The Bible Is Our Standard

When Moses wanted direction and to know the way of the Lord, He went to God directly and asked for His word. He understood that power resides in God's word. While we can't meet with God physically as Moses could, we do have another means of understanding His heart. The ways of the Lord are accurately, clearly, and fully recorded in Scripture. You want to know God? You want to discern His voice from your own? Get to know His written Word.

Scripture touches on every aspect of our lives, from finances to family matters. God wove a valuable collection of guidelines and life-instruction throughout it. If you are truly hungry for God's direction, you must also be hungry for His Word.

Without a standard to gauge our communication with Him, you and I can easily fall into error about what God directs us to do. We must remember that God's spoken word can always be backed up by His written Word. Individuals who "hear from God" without taking time to verify the message against Scripture risk falling into grave error.

We are imperfect humans trying to hear from a perfect God. Even the most well-intentioned individuals who desire to obey God can misunderstand His instructions. The problem is not with God's communication skills; the problem is with our ability to listen clearly.

You could compare us to a satellite dish that collects a signal to provide clear television reception. Sometimes weather can interfere with the reception thus affecting the ability of the dish to provide a clear picture. Sin and distractions disturb our ability to get strong spiritual signals, thus scrambling our reception. The confusion and chaos of work, family, finances, sin, and even traditionalism can prevent us from clearly hearing God's voice.

What "environmental elements" in your life right now might affect your ability to clearly hear God's voice?

_____

DAILY BREAD

All Scripture is inspired by God and is profitable for teaching, for rebuking, for correcting, for training in righteousness, so that the man of God may be complete, equipped for every good work.
2 Timothy 3:16-17

God's spoken word can *always* be backed up by His written Word.

Every part of Scripture is God-breathed and useful one way or another—showing us truth, exposing our rebellion, correcting our mistakes, training us to live God's way. Through the Word we are put together and shaped up for the tasks God has for us.
2 Timothy 3:16-17, The Message

Many things clamor for our attention when life gets busy. Our emotions fluctuate. Our friends and families demand our time and energy. Hearing God's voice in the midst of the chaos can be difficult. Scripture descrambles the distortion by either authenticating or disproving what we think we have heard.

The Bible Is Absolute Truth

God will *never* give us fresh spoken words that contradict His written Word. He will not give us instructions that do not align with Scripture. God's absolute standards are revealed only in His Word.

The Bible alone provides the foundational directives you and I need to make decisions that glorify God. Apart from reliance on the truth of Scripture, we cannot clearly hear Him. Read how *The Message* explains 2 Timothy 3:16-17 (in the margin).

According to this passage, how much of Scripture is inspired by God?

_____

If "every part" of Scripture is God's truth, how should we respond to its words and instructions?

_____

Think carefully about a major decision you might soon make. Which of the following honestly expresses your biggest concern in making that decision?
❑ I worry what my friends/family might say about my choice.
❑ I am concerned as to which option is the most convenient.
❑ I wonder which decision might prove the most personally profitable.
❑ I'm curious to know what Scripture says about my situation.

While I can relate to all these concerns, I must always adjust my personal decisions to line up with Scripture. I'm not always good at this, but the more I learn about the Bible, the better I become. For instance, I'm sometimes tempted to press Jerry on a certain issue, but when I consider the Bible's warnings about nagging women (Prov. 21:9,19; 1 Peter 3:1-2) I squelch my desire to fuss at my husband. I've passed up many opportunities that would be fun yet time consuming because Ephesians 5:16 reminds me to make the most of my time.

Describe a time when Scripture's truth has changed your decisions.

_____

_____

The foundation for hearing God speak is knowing and believing in the absolute truth of the Bible. We must not only recognize Scripture as God's truth, we must obey it.

Read Proverbs 3:5-6. What does it mean to "not rely on your own understanding"?

_____

When we devote ourselves to reading Scripture, it becomes a part of us, reminding us of its precepts and encouraging us to obey its guidelines. For instance, a recent family situation bothered me for some time. I found myself complaining about it constantly, but the Holy Spirit convicted me about my negative attitude through two important Scriptures. James 5:9 says, "Do not complain about one another, so that you will not be judged." First Peter 4:9 says that we should "be hospitable to one another without complaining."

Though Scripture's message to me was clear, I didn't immediately stop complaining—at least not until I came across 1 John 2:3-6.

According to 1 John 2:3-6, what is the determining factor that reveals whether or not someone truly knows the Lord? Underline your answer in the margin.

The term *know* as used in verse 4 of 1 John 2 is the Greek word *ginosko*. It means "to know intimately." To "know" someone in this sense is not to just have a casual relationship with them but to know details about them in a way that is special and specific to only the two of you. The closer you get to God the more frequently and readily you will hear and identify the voice of God speaking to you. Intimacy and closeness with Him should be our continuous desire.

If an observer was to evaluate your current decision-making process, what would it reveal about whether or not you truly know the Lord?

_____

Describe a time when you obeyed God in a difficult situation. How did your obedience result in deeper intimacy with Him?

_____

_____

Intimacy with God requires the same time, energy, and effort we put into human friendship. The closer we become to friends the more detailed information we

This is how we are sure that we have come to know Him: by keeping His commands. The one who says, "I have come to know Him," without keeping His commands, is a liar, and the truth is not in him. But whoever keeps His word, truly in him the love of God is perfected. This is how we know we are in Him: the one who says he remains in Him should walk just as He walked.
1 John 2:3-6

"The one who has My commandments and keeps them is the one who loves Me. ... the one who loves Me will be loved by My Father. I also will love him and will reveal Myself to him."
John 14:21.

receive from them about their lives. The more they can trust us the more apt they are to reveal specific and detailed information. In the same way, intimacy with the Father brings increased communication. The closer we are to God the more readily we will hear His voice.

Circle the phrases in John 14:21 that show to whom Christ will reveal Himself.

You have just uncovered one of the great promises of Scripture! Jesus gives you the key to hearing His voice: obey His Word and grow in intimacy with Him.

TAKE ACTION

Renew your commitment to His Word. Lay your hand on the Bible and talk to the Lord. Tell Him that you will trust His words regardless of the way you feel. Renew your commitment to the Bible as the ultimate basis for all your decisions.

DAY 3
Hungry for His Presence

DAILY BREAD
Moses had one more request. "Please let me see your glorious presence." Exodus 33:18, NLT

When Moses said, "Please let me see your glorious presence" (Ex. 33:18), he was *desperate* for the Lord. He could not settle for a marginal relationship with God. He needed more.

Many times Moses had spoken with the Lord. God had faithfully delivered him in the most dramatic fashion we could imagine. Yet Moses needed more than God's victory over his enemies, more than God's power to lead the people, more than physical food and water, and more than another miracle. He wanted to experience the overwhelming presence of the Lord—nothing less would satisfy.

God told Moses to continue his journey into the promised land and that He would continue to protect and provide for the Hebrews along the way. However, these promises included a stunning comment by God.

What did God say in Exodus 33:3-4 that caused the people to mourn?

_____

Can you imagine Moses' distress as God says He will withdraw from the Israelites? Moses didn't just beg God to reconsider His decision; Moses conferenced with Him. Moses sought His counsel. He reminded the Lord that the Hebrews were His chosen people. He declared, "If you don't go with us personally, don't let us move or step from this place." "Please," Moses asked, desperate for divine guidance and direction, "let me see your glorious presence!"

As I imagine the scene, I can almost hear Moses pleading: "Don't give up on us, Lord! I need you. I trust you. Guide me! Meet with me! Lead me!"

God desires followers desperate for His presence: people who don't necessarily want His blessings but want Him! God wants followers like Moses, people who balk at the idea of going anywhere without His leading. Not only is His presence the only means of salvation, it is the only distinguishing characteristic between the followers of God and those who follow different gods (Ex. 33:16).

Those desperate for God realize that only with God's presence can they survive life's journeys. We need to experience the manifest presence of God.

> The following words describe the term *manifest*: obvious, clear, visible, marked, noticeable, observable. How is God's manifest presence different from His omnipresence?

_____

Why God Removes His Presence

In Exodus 33:5 God described the Israelites as "stiff-necked" or "stubborn." Some translations say "hard-hearted." Not much has changed in 3500 years. Time and again, God's people prove by our actions that we are not as concerned with pleasing God as with having our way.

> Circle the words that describe how you feel when you are around a stubborn child.
>
> anxious   angry   impatient   irritable   out of control
> amused   pleased   distracted   loving   other: _____

Like children determined to have things their own way, the Israelites had become obstinate. God decided to remove His presence because of their stubbornness. God knows that His people will sin, but He refuses to bless a place where people are stubborn, rebellious, and set in their own ways. Stubbornness is so offensive to God that it elicits the threat of complete destruction (see Ex. 33:3,5; Deut. 9:8,14).

God becomes especially angered with those who arrogantly continue in their sin when confronted. God will not manifest His presence in a place driven by evil stubbornness and without a genuine thirst for Him. He does not force Himself on us but waits for us to thirst for and desire Him.

Read Deuteronomy 9:6-12 and answer the following questions.

How long had the people been obstinate? (v. 7) _____

How did the Lord respond to their actions at Mt. Horeb? (v. 8)

_____

While the Lord was meeting with Moses on the mountain, the people became impatient. What did the people fill their time doing? (vv. 9-12)

_____

Are you living an obstinate lifestyle before God in any area of your life right now? If so, how?

_____

What idols have you built for yourself? _____

A Matter of the Heart

Stubbornness is an internal issue that can be devastating to our spiritual health. As we discussed in week 3, we cultivate the presence of God in our lives not merely through our actions but through our hearts and attitudes. We must develop continuous humility before Him. If we are not seeing the presence of God in our lives, it may be because we lack a hunger and thirst for Him.

Stubbornness quenches our thirst for God. If you find you do not pant for Him as the deer pants for water (see Ps. 42:1), evaluate yourself to see if you have become stiff-necked. God promises He will meet with those who hunger and thirst for Him (Isa. 41:17).

According to Psalm 42:6, what caused David to be truly thirsty for God?

_____

In all their suffering, He suffered, and the Angel of His Presence saved them. He redeemed them because of His love and compassion; He lifted them up and carried them all the days of the past. Isaiah 63:9

Isn't this typical of us? We don't feel strong desire until God puts us in a position of desperate need. Maybe that's why He refuses to simply show up whenever we call. As we seek God's presence, He may allow us to get extremely thirsty. That thirst will drive us to the living water.

Isaiah 63:9 gives us two critical bits of information for times when God seems to withdraw His presence and allows us to thirst. God shares our affliction, and we find our rescue in His Presence. If we will go to Him, He will give us rest (see Matt. 11:28). Only the Lord can satisfy.

TAKE ACTION

Ask the Lord to forgive any rebellion that keeps you from desperately seeking Him and experiencing His manifest presence. Ask Him to give you a genuine thirst for Him as you seek to follow His plan for your life. Trust in the promise of His Word: He will respond to those who hunger and thirst for Him (Matt. 5:6).

DAY 4
Hungry for His Peace

What actions haunt you with guilt? Keeping the extra change the cashier accidentally gave, rationalizing that the store would never miss a few pennies? A lie to impress? Using feminine charm to manipulate a situation? I plead guilty, and I fear I'm not alone. What should we do when we can't get away from ourselves?

We as Christians have built-in meters to gauge our behavior. The Holy Spirit works in us, continually urging us to check our actions against what we know is right. When we get off track, we may experience guilt or even suffer consequences. But when our lives align with God's plans, we find peace.

Peace is a gift that accompanies salvation. As believers, we are not on a search for peace: it's already in us and available to us. Peace results from God's presence in our lives. It calms, reassures, and comforts. Peace brings rest, tranquility, assuredness, security, and safety. When we experience the lack of quiet rest, we need to ask if our hearts may be sensing the absence of God's presence or approval.

DAILY BREAD

The peace of God, which surpasses every thought, will guard your hearts and your minds in Christ Jesus.
Philippians 4:7

Peace Rules

Recently, my husband and I were at odds about a particular situation, so I did what I thought was appropriate: I kept bringing it up! I did it in a way that seemed very "loving" to me. I put a smile on my face, waited until the appropriate time, and made sure I was not nagging. (At least it didn't sound like nagging to me.)

Outwardly I was confident about my decision to keep discussing the situation, but deep down inside I wasn't at peace. Every time I decided to bring up the issue I felt the Ruler of my heart throw up a warning flag, yet ahead I went. I spoke in a peaceful tone, but I was blatantly ignoring the lack of peace in my heart. As a result, my peace and my marriage both suffered. Colossians 3:15 tells us to "let the peace of Christ rule in your hearts" (NASB).

If you can relate to my story, why do you think we sometimes forge ahead when the Spirit is telling us to stop?

❏ Self-centeredness—we just want our own way.

❏ Blindness—we can't see from other people's perspective.

❏ Stubbornness—we're just not going to give in.

❏ Control—we're afraid to surrender the driver's seat.

❏ Other _____

How can you tell that you either have or lack the peace of Christ?

_____

This week we've studied Moses' requests: "Lord, teach me your ways" (Ex. 33:13). "Please, Lord, don't make us go without You" (v. 15). Each time I read Exodus, I am touched by God's comforting response to Moses' pleas: "My presence will go with you. I will give you rest." God's presence and the rest He provides fit together. Even when God disciplines us, the end result is restored peace.

Our Relationship with Peace

Peace, or the lack thereof, is a crucial component in hearing God's voice and deciphering His will. We may be able to live without it, but who would want to? So what must we do to have God's peace? We need to learn never to take lightly those decisions or plans that leave our hearts in turmoil. When you feel a tug of war ensuing in your heart, pay close attention. Peace or a lack of it can settle a debate or argument for us, leading to correct decisions.

In high school I dated a football player. He was a nice guy but had a reputation for being a trouble maker. One afternoon he invited me to his house. I knew his parents weren't home, but I tried to ignore the fact.

A war ensued in my heart as we prepared to go. A lack of peace overwhelmed me. The Holy Spirit reminded me of my parent's instructions never to go to a boy's home unchaperoned. I went with him anyway.

Within an hour I was face-to-face with the reason the Ruler had warned me. This young man, whom I had known throughout school, became a different person. His boyish charm turned into aggression, leaving me in an awful position.

The Lord spared me from what could have been a horrible outcome. I hurt for the thousands of women who have not been so fortunate. That incident serves as a distinct reminder of the danger of ignoring the Holy Spirit's warning.

Read Psalm 32:3-4. It is a great example of the disturbance a lack of peace can cause. Describe a time when you have gone through a period of turmoil as a result of unconfessed sin.

_____

How did the relief that came with surrender and confession feel?

_____

King David's lack of peace brought a response (see Ps. 32:5). He confessed His sin and returned to the Lord. Soul disquiet should serve as a reminder that we must maintain fellowship with God and restore it if it's compromised.

Signs of False Peace

Let me issue a warning. We can have a feeling of peace when we are outside the will of God. Although we are new creatures in Christ and the Spirit of God dwells in us, we remain humans clothed in flesh. A carnal or backslidden Christian can experience the false peace of a dull conscience.

Consider Jonah's story. God calls the prophet to take the message of repentance to the people in Nineveh (Jonah 1:2). Probably because Nineveh was a threat to Israel, Jonah rebelled and left town.

Read Jonah 1:1-5. What was Jonah able to do in the midst of the storm?

_____

Did you note the biblical irony? Jesus slept in a boat on a stormy sea (Luke 8:23-24). Jonah did the same. Jesus was the incarnate God. Jonah was running from God. We can ignore the voice of God and go on quite comfortably it seems.

The Bible gives us several practical ways to discern God's will and distinguish between true and false peace. These red flags can help us determine if we are outside God's will even when we sleep soundly at night. Let's look at them.

Red Flag #1: *Are we running away?* After receiving difficult instructions from God, Jonah's first action was to run away (Jonah 1:3).

What does it feel like to run from God?

_____

Jonah ran from God's instructions. He was actually willing to "pay a fare" (Jonah 1:3) to shirk his responsibility and escape God's will. While he was physically fleeing from Nineveh to Tarshish, Jonah's real goal was to flee from the Lord's presence. He tried to create as much distance as he could between himself and God.

What does Psalm 139:7-10 suggest about the foolishness of Jonah's logic?

_____

> **No matter where we go—God is there. No matter how we rebel, He is still in charge.**

No matter where we go—God is there. No matter how we rebel, He is still in charge. Jonah learned that lesson the hard way. The storm the Lord allowed that day was no ordinary storm. It was windy, heavy, and tumultuous—so fierce that the ship was about to break up.

Red Flag #2: Are we compensating? We can tell something is wrong internally when we try to fill the void with external things. Most of us could name a time when we've tried to fill an inner void with some substance or behavior.

What tells you you're trying to fill a void?
- ❑ the craziness of the busys
- ❑ chocolate, give me chocolate
- ❑ anger looking for an object
- ❑ the need to control
- ❑ an inability to be alone
- ❑ the need for attention
- ❑ which way to the pity party?
- ❑ food, bring me food
- ❑ other_____

We do all these things in an effort to escape the lack of peace inside. But no matter where we go, with whom, or in what exciting diversions, the gnawing need remains. Real peace comes from within. It will not come until we repent before the Lord, seek His will, and begin to walk in it.

Red Flag #3: Are we thankful? Did you notice the last words of Colossians 3:15? Not only are we to allow Christ's peace to rule in our hearts but we are to "be thankful." Thanksgiving is always connected to the outpouring of God's peace.

How do your actions demonstrate your thankfulness to God?

_____

God's peace allows you to have gratitude and thanksgiving in your heart, in your mind, and on your lips. Have you noticed that thankfulness may have nothing to do with circumstances? The Spirit can give you thankfulness for the surprising ways He helps you cope despite your surroundings. When peace rules in your heart, there will be thankfulness and praise on your lips.

God's Persistent Presence

When your circumstances become stormy or unmanageable, you could be experiencing God's intervention. Perhaps He is allowing the trials of life to rouse you from a sense of false peace, to seek the true peace that only comes from Him. The peace God offers brings unity to the entire body of believers. The closer a believer is to Christ, the closer that believer will be to her brothers and sisters in the Lord. Even better, inner peace brings us into closer relationship with God—better preparing us to hear His voice. The more we hunger for His peace, the more we will be able to hear His voice and discern His will.

TAKE ACTION

God gives us peace as a means through which we can discover His leading and follow His ways. When you and I walk in God's will, peace will rule our hearts regardless of our circumstances. In making decisions that glorify God, we must constantly ask, "Am I experiencing God's peace regarding this decision?"

Be honest with God. Are you running from Him? If you are, He is aware of it. According to Proverbs 15:11, the actions of your heart are already laid bare before Him. Confess your desire to flee from Him. Ask Him for His presence and peace.

DAY 5
Hungry for His Power

Today we'll join Moses' quest to discover the power of God. If we want to draw near to God in the ways we have discussed throughout this study, we must have God's power.

As Moses negotiated with God, he said other nations would recognize the uniqueness of God's people because of the Lord's presence (see Ex. 33:16). The passage does not spell out just what the other nations would see, but I think we can make an educated guess. God's power makes His presence evident.

DAILY BREAD

Don't get drunk with wine, which leads to reckless actions, but be filled with the Spirit.
Ephesians 5:18

Read 1 Samuel 4:1-7. To what did both the Israelites and the Philistines respond?

_____

You could have given two answers. You could have said the ark of the covenant or the presence of God because the two were linked. The ark of the covenant represented the manifest presence of God to the children of Israel.

What promise did God's presence include according to Exodus 34:11?

_____

For the Israelites, victory was secure as long as the presence of God was near. They understood that God's presence equals God's power. The same truth applies for us. Without the presence and power of God, we cannot conquer our enemies.

The ancients viewed the ark of the covenant as representing God's presence. The ark itself is currently lost to history, but God's presence is not. God manifests His awesome presence through the power of the Holy Spirit.

When you and I committed our lives to Jesus Christ, we received the Holy Spirit as a pledge of the covenant between us and God. If you have accepted Christ, you have the Holy Spirit. He is a gift.

God's presence equals God's power.

The Holy Spirit's residence in our lives makes it possible for us to walk as victorious Christians. Though we can't physically see the Spirit, the effects of His presence are visible.

Match the following passages to the description of the Spirit's work.

___ gives us everything we need to live godly lives   a. John 16:13
___ convicts us of our sin   b. John 14:26
___ teaches us what Jesus said   c. 2 Peter 1:3
___ guides us into all truth   d. John 16:8

The Spirit is always working as an invisible source inside us. The word *power* summarizes what the Holy Spirit brings to the believer (Acts 1:8). He enables us to live and act as we could not on our own. Through Him we can exhibit love, joy, peace, patience, kindness, faithfulness, gentleness, goodness, and self control —even in those situations that make us want to rage or cry (see Gal. 5:22-23).

Fill in the left side of the chart with tasks you feel incapable of completing in your own power. On the right, explain how you might handle the situation under the Spirit's influence. I have given a few examples to get you started.

In my power, I cannot ...	With the Spirit's power, I can ...
Balance work, family, exercise	Prioritize according to God's priorities
Stop complaining	Quietly and patiently trust in the Lord

We cannot please God without divine resources. How many of us as wives can willingly subject ourselves to our husband's authority without the Spirit's help (see Eph. 5:22-23)? How many husbands can love their wives with the kind of love Christ loves the church (see 5:25)? How many children can submit to parents without the help of the Spirit (see Eph. 6:1-3)? How many parents can deal with their children in a loving way and rear them well without the help of the Holy Spirit (Eph. 6:4)? How can employees submit to the demands of a difficult employer with a smile without an internal source of power (see Eph. 6:6-9)?

God has already given His children everything we need for godliness; the Holy Spirit and the power He brings are included. You received all of the Holy Spirit you are ever going to receive at the moment you became a believer in Christ. Just as God gave Moses the power to continue His journey to the promised land, you and I have power to journey through this Christian life.

Filled Full

God gave every Christian the Spirit at the moment of salvation (see Ro God's Spirit lives in us (see 1 Cor. 3:16, 6:19). We need the full power the Holy Spirit can bring. When we are "filled up" or controlled by the presence and power of the Holy Spirit, it will show in our actions.

In Ephesians 5:14-18 Paul makes reference to Christians who are spiritually asleep. As Christians we can unwisely and foolishly choose to live without a passion for spiritual things. Though the Spirit dwells in us, it is up to us to tap into the benefits He provides.

1. unhealthy college relationships
2. lack of patience with my children
3. usurping authority in my marriage

Write 3 key words or phrases that symbolize foolish decisions you've made as a result of being spiritually asleep. I've listed mine in the margin.

1. _____

2. _____

3. _____

We can go through seasons where we spiritually sleepwalk—not experiencing the Spirit's power. We can never function to our full potential unless we access the power the Spirit provides.

Being "filled with all the fullness of God" (Eph. 3:19) is a work God does for us. We must depend on Him. Our part is to be hungry for His power. Hungry people do whatever is necessary to be filled. When we show God spiritual hunger, He responds.

Really Changed

We ought to see a change when we're filled with the Spirit and under the influence of His power. To be filled with the Spirit simply means to be controlled by the Spirit. When something controls us, it changes the way we think and act and gives us the power to do things we might not normally have the power to do. Scripture provides us a parallel drawn from the physical world.

With what does Ephesians 5:18 contrast being filled with the Spirit?

_____

How does too much alcohol change a person's personality?

_____

When someone is "drunk with wine" they do things they would not normally do. Normally quiet and reserved people can become obnoxious and loud. People who would not normally try to sing may belt out songs without reservation.

What fears might a person filled with the Holy Spirit overcome?

_____

In Ephesians 5 Paul illustrates the change being filled with the Spirit makes. I've broken verses 19 to 21 up into phrases so you can't miss them.
- speaking to one another in psalms and hymns and spiritual songs;
- singing and making music to the Lord;
- always giving thanks for all things in the name of Jesus Christ;
- being subject to one another in the fear of Christ.

Those are pretty major changes for most of us. I know I wouldn't naturally act in those ways apart from the power of the Spirit.

TAKE ACTION

This week we've looked at hunger. It's easy to be hungry for food, but I want to hunger for Christ. I want to hunger for His direction, His presence, His peace, and His power.

Close out the week by asking God to make you hungry and thirsty for Him. Write your prayer below.

_____

_____

_____

_____

Viewer Guide
Session 6

The LORD came and stood and called as at other times, "Samuel!
Samuel!" And Samuel said, **"Speak, for Thy servant is listening."**
—Samuel 3:10

Samuel was a _____.

_____ is the heart of servanthood.

He poured water into the basin, and began to wash the disciples' feet,
and to wipe them with the towel with which He was girded.
—John 13:5

To be a true servant of God you have to be willing to:

- leave your own _____

  and _____ behind

- remove the _____

- take up your _____

Being a servant is not about your _____, it's about your _____.

A Servant Spirit

SHE WAS 15 YEARS OLD when she gave her life to the Lord. While visiting a Christian camp she told the Lord she was committed to being His servant, with one exception. She didn't want to be a pastor's wife.

Three years later at a revival she met the man who would be her husband. Their lives began and took them through Bible college and seminary. She was excited about a life of ministry with her husband until he announced that God was calling him to be a pastor. This was the one thing she didn't want to do with her life. It took two years to accept and yield to God's plan for her.

My mother, Lois Evans, has been a pastor's wife for 30 years now. She and my father, Tony, have ministered faithfully to a congregation that has grown to over 7,000 people. Now she realizes this is what God had in mind all along. Her ministry is not just to her congregation but to other pastors' wives across the world.

A true servant of God must be willing to surrender to God's plan completely. Godly servanthood means laying aside our desires in full pursuit of His.

DAY 1
Submissive to the Lord's Assignment

We find true peace and contentment when we submit to God's assignment. To understand and accept the callings or assignments God has for us, we must first understand that we have been set up.

Turn to Ephesians 2:10 and fill in the blank below:

We are His creation—created in Christ Jesus for good works,

_____ that we should walk in them."

From the beginning of time, our life-purposes have been planned. God assigned us to do great things for His kingdom, now we just have to walk in His purpose.

My sister, you were not placed in your family, in your neighborhood, or on your job by accident. Your existence is God-planned. Your past, present, and future are in His hands. Let this knowledge inspire you to present yourself, as Samuel did, to God's pre-planned assignment for you.

Gifted for His Purposes

Jeremiah 1:4-5 clearly states that before we were even conceived, we were on God's mind. He created each of us, setting us aside for a specific purpose. As Christians, no matter our professions, we are called to serve in God's kingdom.

We have the privilege of fulfilling God's purposes. We can have confidence in submitting to God's assignments, when we first understand that we each have gifts: specific abilities to grow and bless the kingdom of God.

Read 1 Corinthians 12:4-11. Where do spiritual gifts originate (v. 4)?

_____

DAILY BREAD

God ... has ... called us with a holy calling, not according to our works, but according to His own purpose and grace, which was given to us in Christ Jesus before time began.
2 Timothy 1:8-9

No matter our specific gifts, all can be used to minister. Actively using our gifts for God's glory fulfills our callings. The word *gift* implies that we neither select nor deserve these by our own merit. Our gifts are an extension of God's grace, delightful treasures we are to enjoy and invest back into the kingdom of God. Sometimes, however, we use our gifts for personal reward.

When I first began speaking, I learned that motivational speakers are in high demand. As one of two female speakers with the Zig Ziglar Corporation and the only African American speaker, I was one of those highly requested presenters. I was paid top dollar to stand before an audience in a corporate setting. But after several years of traveling as a motivational speaker, I sensed growing personal dissatisfaction. I closed seminars feeling unfulfilled. I wanted to do more than make an audience laugh: I wanted their lives to be changed. My bank account grew larger while my spirit grew less satisfied.

I asked the Lord about those feelings, wondering what I was doing wrong. Perhaps I wasn't meant to speak. Dozens of scenarios flew through my mind, leaving me empty and discouraged. Then one day the Lord spoke to my heart. He affirmed that He'd given me the gift of public speaking but pointed out that I was using the talent for my own benefit rather than His kingdom.

Over the next months I discovered that with each corporate event I accepted, the Holy Spirit tugged at my thoughts: "Stop riding your own dreams, Priscilla. Ride the tide of My plan for you." I struggled to give up my will and obey God's leading. But God continued to speak to me through Scripture, patiently bending me to His purposes by revealing His perspective.

My heart transition began when I read 2 Corinthians 5:1-9. Paul's life ambition was to please God because he knew and understood that "the earthly tent" or the things of this earth are only temporary. Paul focused his attention on that which is eternal. What a powerful reminder for me that my gifts had been given to fulfill His assignment. I simply needed to submit to it.

According to 2 Corinthians 5:20, what is the role of an ambassador?

_____

How can you be an ambassador for God right where you are?

_____

I'd become an ambassador of Priscilla instead of an ambassador for the Lord. Making money had become more important to me than being a part of the eternal purpose He had for my life.

Check a number to indicate how important each of the following is to you. Five represents the most important and 1 represents the least.

	1	2	3	4	5
Achieving excellence in my career	❏	❏	❏	❏	❏
Pleasing Christ	❏	❏	❏	❏	❏
Making money	❏	❏	❏	❏	❏
Getting married	❏	❏	❏	❏	❏
Being a good mother	❏	❏	❏	❏	❏

Nothing is wrong with making money, getting married, or having children. Those things, however, are temporary. You and I are here for more than the temporary happiness earthly things provide. When you understand and accept your God-given assignment and begin to utilize your gifts to fulfill it, you will find contentment this world cannot provide.

God may not call you to full-time ministry, but He may call you to alter the way you function as a business woman, wife, or mother.

What duties does your job require?

_____

What gifts has God given you that make that position a good fit for you?

_____

How does living for God's purpose change the way you do your job?

_____

How can you fulfill God's purposes in your current job?

_____

Copy these statements onto a note card. Carry it with you and repeat them several times a day.

- My life means more than the temporary.
- I live at this point in history for a reason.
- My existence is no mistake.
- I'm here for a purpose, to fulfill my God-given role!

TAKE ACTION

I love to think of our personal "callings" as invitations to be part of something divine. When I am invited to a friend's house for dinner or a party, I don't go over and try to run things. I don't plan dinner, set the table, invite the guests, clean up the house, or take over the program. My part, as the invitee, is simply to show up, go with the flow, and enjoy the festivities.

God has invited us to be part of something great. Our duty is to participate in what He has planned. Scripture says, "We know that all things work together for the good of those who love God: those who are called according to His purpose" (Rom. 8:28). With this in mind, let's decide to willingly go along with God's plans instead of our own.

The Lord does not and will not make us do anything. He will invite us, and we will be blessed as we submit to His calling on our lives.

Close your study time in prayer. Honestly tell the Lord your response to His invitation to live for Him. Ask Him to use your gifts for His glory.

DAY 2
Submissive to the Lord's Challenges

The day before I wrote this lesson I felt tired, frustrated, and overwhelmed as Jerry, Jackson, and I flew home from a trip to Atlanta. After waking up early to get myself and the rest of the family to the airport on time, I was exhausted. My second pregnancy made me feel perpetually sleepy.

My exhaustion didn't matter to my son as he excitedly explored the airport in search of fun. When we boarded the plane, he was even more excited. He played and laughed with the people sitting in front of and behind him, so I had to stay alert every minute of the one-hour delay and two-hour flight.

Once we got home, dinner needed to be made, clothes needed to be washed, and Jackson needed a bath. As I finally landed in bed, I wondered: *How did I get myself into this?* But as my head hit the pillow, the Lord reminded me that my family is my first ministry—my divine assignment. Caring for them fulfills part of God's call on my life.

Multiple demands often leave us feeling as if we have more then we can handle. Yesterday we talked about what it means to accept God's assignment and yield to His desires by delighting in Him. Today we focus on the fact that God's assignments do not come free from challenges. On the contrary, hard times often come, either derailing us from the mission or making us stronger and more committed to following through with what God asks of us.

DAILY BREAD

"In this world you will have trouble. But take courage. I have overcome the world."
John 16:33, NIV

John 16:33 verifies that we will find suffering and trials in this life, but it also offers encouragement. Jesus has conquered the world. Through the power of His Holy Spirit, we too can triumph over difficulty.

Which of the following emotions do you normally experience when facing trouble? Underline all that apply.

shock	frustration	anger	acceptance
sadness	depression	irritation	peace

What encouragement do you find in 1 Peter 4:12-13 concerning trouble?

_____

Trials and challenges are inevitable. We must learn to expect them, submit to them and learn from them. However, we can rest assured that behind every challenge we can find God. He orchestrates the events of our lives to build us up and bring Himself glory, but that doesn't mean we will always like what He has assigned us to do. We often encounter great challenges as we walk in obedience to God. The greatest challenge of all might just be getting used to the fact that sometimes His assignments are different than the plans we had for ourselves.

Choose three of the following examples. List the challenges these individuals faced while following God's assignments. Then briefly explain how God built them up or brought Himself glory through their situations.

Abraham—Genesis 22:12   Mary—Luke 1:28-34
Jeremiah—Jeremiah 1:5-7   Moses—Exodus 7:1-4; 14:8-12
David—1 Samuel 17:41-44;19:9-10 Esther—Esther 8:3-4
Paul and Silas—Acts 16:22-23   Stephen—Acts 7:57-59

Challenge   Resulting Glory

We can't choose all aspects of our God-given assignments. We will probably always dislike some parts of what God calls us to do, but we can control our responses. We can rejoice in the good we know God will bring from hardship, and we can rejoice in the Lord Himself even when no good seems possible. Here are some reasons why.

We must learn to see challenges as spiritual exercises designed to make us stronger.

A Matter of Perspective

As we submit to the Lord's plans, we must first allow God to change our perspective, radically realigning our desires with His. The challenges we face are not meant to destroy us. They are designed to make us more capable of fulfilling our God-given assignments. We must learn to see challenges as spiritual exercises designed to make us stronger.

Look at James 1:2-4. What attributes does God build through trials?

_____

The Greek word used for the word "trial" in James is *peirasmos*. This word means "experiment." The goal of an experiment is to validate a hypothesis or to experientially validate a set of theories that have not yet been proven true. God sometimes wants to demonstrate to us truth about ourselves or Himself. Only through trials do we move from theoretical to practical faith.

How could viewing challenges as exercises given by your loving Father help to change your perspective on hardship?

_____

Consider it a great joy, my brothers, whenever you experience various trials, knowing that the testing of your faith produces endurance. But endurance must do its complete work, so that you may be mature and complete, lacking nothing.
James 1:2-4

Let the Lord change your perspective and begin to see life's challenges as a help instead of a hindrance. You may still experience times of frustration, but a new perspective will change the way you handle negative feelings. Peter and the apostles continued in obedience to their God-given assignment in the face of many challenges and hardships. In fact, because they would not dismiss their calling and continued to preach the gospel of Jesus, they were brutally beaten.

What was their emotional response to this trial? (see Acts 5:41)

_____

These men changed their outlook and perspective on the challenges they faced. They knew that obedience to God was more important than pleasing men or protecting their own comfort and safety (see Acts 5:29).

What challenges are you currently facing?

_____

What life lessons are your current challenges teaching you?

_____

_____

Knowing our challenges are developing character enables us to change our emotional response to trials. As I consider the flight back from Atlanta, I remember God uses even my most frustrating days to build me into the woman He wants me to be. When I am weak He is strong (see 2 Cor. 12:10).

A Matter of Focus

We need to keep our eyes focused on eternity, always remembering God is in control. In light of the great reward that awaits those who suffer for the sake of Christ, our challenges shrink.

What is your greatest struggle right now—a relationship, children, finances? Keep your eyes focused on eternity. Remember this is not your home. You are simply passing through on your way to your true residence in heaven! Second Corinthians 4:17 says that "our momentary light affliction is producing for us an absolutely incomparable eternal weight of glory."

I can so easily become bogged down in trials, schedules, and diaper changes that I sometimes forget God sees my efforts as service to Him. He is actually preparing a magnificent place of rest and reward for me. On days when things get rough, I'm wise to temporarily take my eyes off the mess in the kitchen and focus instead on eternity. Times do come when I get so concerned with life's messes that I panic and try desperately to fix the problems on my own. In the process, I can forget about heaven altogether.

I once heard speaker Cal Thomas illustrate this well. He explained that if he were on vacation and staying in a hotel room where he didn't like the decor or carpet, it would be silly for him to get frustrated and upset and call the manager to complain about his surroundings. It would be a much better use of his time and energy to simply endure the ugly decor and remember that he is only passing through. He won't stay in the hotel forever. Soon he will be in the comfort of home. Keep your eyes focused on your real home: heaven. Don't get so frustrated with life that you forget you are passing through.

Rewrite Philippians 3:20 in one sentence or less using your own words.

_____

In the margin, note at least one Scripture to share with your group that helps you remember to keep an eternal perspective.

A Matter of Security

We need to remember that God will never abandon us. When we are burdened, broken, and in need, He reminds us we are not alone. God will not only never leave our side, He watches over us and knows when enough is enough.

What trade name does Malachi 3:3 give God?
❏ cobbler   ❏ silversmith   ❏ blacksmith

The refiner desires to bring forth the metal in its truest form. To do this, he places the object in the fire and carefully observes its response to the heat. The silversmith watches the metal, prepared to take it out at just the right moment. Too much heat will damage the precious work.

God is the divine silversmith refining metal to rid it of impurities. When we are burdened, broken, and in need, He reminds us we are not alone. God will not only never leave our side, He watches over us and knows when enough is enough.

Do you know how the silversmith knows the refining process is complete? He must be able to clearly see his reflection in the molten metal. We sometimes find ourselves in a place we believe is too difficult. The intense heat seems to be too much to bear, but God is paying close attention. His work will be done and we will be ready when He can see His reflection in us.

In what ways have your challenges made you more Christlike?

_____

TAKE ACTION

First Thessalonians 5:18 says that we should give thanks in everything! We can purposefully turn our attention to God and thank Him for what He is doing in our lives even through trials. Close your time of Bible study today with your own personal thanksgiving service. Think carefully about the current challenges you face and give thanks to God especially for those things. Thank Him for how He is using those as experiments to build you up and that you can count on His presence to be with you through the whole thing! Thank Him for heaven and the promise of eternity with Him.

DAY 3
Submissive to the Lord's Desires

When I first met my husband, I tried to set him up—with my sister! Why? He didn't immediately match my desires. But as I opened myself to what God wanted for me, my desires changed. My feelings for Jerry grew and became a consuming passion. Once I became hungry and desperate for the Lord's desires in my life instead of my own, the Lord placed His desire in my heart and now my desires match His.

DAILY BREAD

Delight yourself in the LORD; And He will give you the desires of your heart.
Psalm 37:4, NASB

Carefully consider the deep truth of Psalm 37:4. What must we do to receive our "hearts' desires"?

_____

The Hebrew word used for "delight" in Psalm 37:4 is *anag*. It means "to make merry over, to take exquisite delight." Throughout Scripture "delighting" requires an inner fervor. Delighting in God is a natural reaction from enthusiastic, spiritually hungry, and passionate people so in love with God that they want to please Him in every way.

Name something or someone in which you truly find delight.

_____

How would an onlooker know you delight in that person or object?

_____

When we are delighted, it shows. Delight always provokes a response. Delighting ourselves in the Lord results in action. We aren't delighting in God if we aren't doing something about it.

Each of the following examples depicts men who delighted themselves in God. What happened as a result of their focus?

Daniel 3:15-18,27 _____

Nehemiah 1:11–2:8 _____

Acts 12:5-7 _____

Acts 16:22-30 _____

Delight and Righteousness

Psalm 37:4 says that when we delight in the Lord He will grant us the desires of our hearts. When we delight in Him, we develop the kind of righteous desires God wants to grant. When God truly becomes our heart's delight, we desire what He wants for us.

Note that desire follows rather than precedes delighting in God. The psalmist does not ask us if we want to delight ourselves in the Lord. He does not invite us to delight ourselves in the Lord when circumstances permit. Rather, he commands that we do it.

If God granted our desires without our delighting in Him first, there's no telling what we would ask for! Most often, our desires would lead us in the wrong direction and we would miss God's best.

What does Psalm 84:11 promise? Underline your answer in the margin.

God responds to lawful, good, and righteous desires. They fit into His sovereign plan for our lives and His kingdom. Apart from an intimate relationship with God a human heart desires sinful things. My angry heart seeks revenge and my lustful heart brings to my mind compromising situations. When I am on the outskirts of a bountiful and delightful relationship with God and not making it my conscious and consuming effort to remain close to Him in obedience, I find that my heart desires the very things that are contrary to what God would desire for me.

Recall a time when your relationship with God was lacking. How did your desires evidence this fact?

_____

_____

_____

For the Lord God is a sun and shield. The Lord gives grace and glory; He does not withhold the good from those who live with integrity. Psalm 84:11

Our desires most closely align themselves with His when we are delighting in Him. The closer we are to Him the more our hearts desire to please Him. Then as we begin to express to Him what our hearts long for, He can gladly answer. We find ourselves praying back to Him the very things He wants for us. What father wouldn't grant the request of a child who requests what the parent wants to give anyway (see Matt. 7:11)?

Jackson knows he can please me by eating his vegetables. When we are having one of those cuddly and sweet Mommy-Jackson times right before lunch or dinner, he will make a point of slowly reaching for his squash, green beans, or carrots. He wants to make sure that I see his effort to please.

Likewise, when you and the Lord have intimate times, your heart will so desire to please Him that you will desire what He desires. You will become more concerned with how your "diet" is pleasing to God than how it pleases you.

I am amazed how this truth makes itself evident in my own life. It surprises me how drastically my desires change and conform to a completely different standard when I am wrapped up in God. When I delight in Him, the rebel in me desires to submit, the stressed mother in me desires to be more patient, and the jealous sister in me desires to befriend the target of her jealousy.

Delighting ourselves in God rolls out the red carpet for God to march right in and plant His good, acceptable, and perfect desires in our hearts so that we can get busy praying them and getting some answers. David knew this to be true. In Psalm 20:4-5, he prayed for victory over enemies and that God would grant the petition of His people, but he buffered his prayer requests with the reasons God should show them favor. For additional Scripture examples of obedience preceding blessing, study the following passages: Psalm 37:4-5,27,34; Isaiah 58:14; James 4:7; 1 Peter 5:6.

We can be so sure that every detail in our lives of love for God is worked into something good. Romans 8:28, The Message.

Delight and Contentment

Do not be afraid to hunger for the desires of the Lord to fill your heart. Not only are God's desires better than our own, but we will find more complete contentment with His plan. When you allow God to renew your mind, a fresh desire for Him will lead to a plan you will love!

I began today's study by telling how my desires about Jerry changed as I delighted myself in the Lord. Please understand this critical point, I didn't marry Jerry because I felt God wanted me to. On the contrary, God changed my desire. I began to long for him like I had no other before. I desperately wanted to be his wife. Now that we have been married for some time, I can see why the Lord wanted us together. He has done some amazing things in both our lives that I would not have been able to accomplish without Jerry's personality and characteristics. The Lord aligned my fleshly desires with His righteous ones to achieve His greater goal in both of our lives.

TAKE ACTION

Be honest with the Lord. Tell Him how you feel about Him. Ask Him to give you the inner fervor to delight in Him. Express to Him your desperation to know and understand His desires for you. Submit your desires and look forward to them changing to match His.

DAY 4
Submissive to the Lord's Authority

The word *submission* sends most of us reeling! It conjures images of door mats and prison bars. We don't like submission, and we don't want to submit. Perhaps we don't even know how. But if we want to hear God's voice and experience His best, we must learn to willingly submit to His authority.

First, look at the meaning of the word *submit* as it appears in Scripture. The Greek word used for submit is *huppotasso*. It means "to subject one's self or to yield to authority." As a woman I want to stress that God calls everyone to submit. Everyone has to answer to many different authorities.

DAILY BREAD

"I want you to know that Christ is the head of every man, and the man is the head of the woman, and God is the head of Christ."
I Corinthians 11:3

Carefully read each of the following verses and for each check whether the author is speaking to males, females, married women or men, or both.

	Males	Females	Married	Both
1 Peter 5:5				
James 4:7				
Hebrews 13:17				
1 Peter 2:18				
Ephesians 5:22				
Romans 13:1				
Ephesians 6:1				

The process of submitting begins with a personal commitment to willingly and gladly follow the authority placed in our lives. Just as we must decide to obey a yield sign, we must choose and commit to submission. The term does not imply something forced on us but a willingness on our part to yield. In fact, how we respond to those God places in authority over us directly indicates how well we'll respond to God's authority. You may have been surprised to discover that only one of the passages on submission deals with married women.

Submission does not imply something forced on us but a willingness on our part to yield.

Look back to 1 Samuel 3:1-10 for a great example of submission. Three times Samuel thought Eli was calling for him. What does Samuel's response tell us about his general response to authority (see v. 5)?

_____

Eli was old and losing his vision (v. 2). Someone in Samuel's position might have thought senility was kicking in and neglected to respond. Yet Samuel was submissive to the authority placed over him. He willingly went to the priest three times. His submission to earthly authority indicated what God could expect when giving direct instructions. Could this have been the reason God chose to speak to Samuel?

Name the authorities God has placed over you.

_____

What might your submission to their authority show God about how you will respond to Him?

_____

_____

Our Problem with Submission

I've always had a rebellious streak against authority. When I am given a leader, my first instinct is to rebel against him or her. As a teenager I rebelled against my parents, and I rebelled against college assignments. I tried to skirt the strong guidelines set up by my seminary, and I've often seen this rebellious streak rear its head in my marriage.

Why is the foundational principle of submission so difficult? The answer is found in two words: human nature! Romans 8:7 calls it "the flesh." We want to have our own way, and we become angry and resentful when we don't get it.

Nothing in us as humans desires to bend under the authority of another. In fact, since the beginning of time, rebellion has been a problem: When she ate the fruit in the garden, Eve rebelled against God (Gen. 3:2-6). Satan wants to turn us against God by taking His authority.

Our deep-rooted desire to sin keeps us from subjecting ourselves to God's leadership. But our freedom and contentment comes when we submit to God's authority. That means submission to human authorities is a lifestyle choice. We must learn to see submission as a positive designed for our good.

On a cold day I love to sit in front of a fire with a warm cup of hot chocolate. The flames bring warmth, brightness, and a sense of peace into my home. The fire is no less of a fire because it is contained, but it flourishes and brings contentment because of its boundaries. If that same fire were allowed outside of the fireplace, it could destroy my house. The fire I loved and appreciated would become my enemy.

Submission is the art of learning to remain "in the fireplace." Once we step outside of the boundaries God sets for us, we too begin to harm our environment. Safety, freedom, and enjoyment come when we live within the bounds of the authority God has placed in our lives.

How does viewing submission as a gift for our good rather than a loss of freedom change your attitude toward it?

_____

_____

What other picture describes the benefits of submission? Think about this and plan to discuss it in your group.

_____

_____

_____

Submission is not a negative. We have simply grown accustomed to believing Satan's lies about it. We must realize that a refusal to follow the authority God has placed in our lives is, in essence, a refusal to follow God.

Submission in Marriage

Many volumes have been written on the thorny problem of submission in marriage. No one answer will fit every situation, so let me emphasize *attitude*. First Peter reminds us as wives to "be submissive to your own husbands so that even if any of them are disobedient to the word, they may be won without a word by the behavior of their wives, as they observe your chaste and respectful behavior" (1 Peter 3:1-2, NASB).

Pay double attention to that word *respectful*. Aretha Franklin wasn't the only one who wanted r-e-s-p-e-c-t. In recent years some counselors have recognized respect from his wife is a husband's greatest need. Scriptural submission does not mean blind obedience, but even if we cannot follow our husbands in action, we can display an attitude of respect.

A willing attitude is the biggest part of submission not only for wives but for everyone. If you submit to authority but with a disgruntled attitude, then you can be sure you will do the same when God calls for you. The main reason we submit has nothing to do with being a woman. It is because Christ Himself was willing to submit.

The main reason we submit is because Christ Himself was willing to submit.

I love how Paul explains the surprising magnitude of Christ's humility in Philippians 2:6-8: "Who, although He existed in the form of God, did not regard equality with God a thing to be grasped, but emptied Himself, taking the form of a bond-servant, and being made in the likeness of men, being found in appearance as a man, He humbled Himself by becoming obedient to the point of death, even death on a cross" (NASB).

TAKE ACTION

In those times when you struggle to submit, remember that no earthly leader is the final authority on any matter. God is. Submit to others to please Him.

Write key principles from today's lesson that inspired you. Ask yourself, "What will I do as a result of what I've learned today?"

_____

_____

DAY 5
Submissive to the Lord's Timing

DAILY BREAD

For you have need of endurance (patience), so that when you have done the will of God you may receive what was promised.
Hebrews 10:36

I set out on this journey asking God, "what must I do to put myself in a position to hear from You?" Again and again I've had to confront the reality that, while I can put myself in position to hear from God, I cannot make Him speak. God's timing is perfect. Of all the things God has asked of me, this has been the hardest: doing nothing as I wait for Him.

For our final day's study let's turn our attention to the prophet Habakkuk. This prophet lived in a day when Israel's enemies were both evil and overwhelming. He could not understand how God could allow enemies to take over His people. Habakkuk cried out for help and anxiously waited for God's response. The prophet was so anxious to hear from God that he compared his stance to that of a soldier stationed on a watchtower (Hab. 2:1). Habakkuk desperately longed to hear God's voice, and he was fully prepared to make whatever response was needed.

As I think about what I want to take away from this experience of studying God's word, Habakkuk serves as my model. His stance was militant, his determination strong, and his resolve sure. Above all else he determined to wait for God's response. And I wish for you, my sister, just such determination.

Which of the following best describes your "stance" as you await God's fresh words for you?

❏ militant   ❏ impatient

❏ nonchalant   ❏ patient

I want to be like Habakkuk as I wait to hear from God. But I'm impatient. Graciously waiting is not one of my strengths. Whether I am hungry and waiting on a meal, sitting in an airplane terminal waiting on a delayed flight, or waiting on God to make good on a promise, I hate delays. But often the wait in seeing God's plans for us revealed demands that we exhibit patience.

Paraphrase Habakkuk 2:3 in the margin.

God warns Habakkuk, "you must be patient. What I am about to tell you is a vision that has an appointed time to come to fulfillment. Don't try to rush it, just relax in knowing that it will not fail!"

My sister, often God also commands us to wait. As He reveals His plans for us, offers challenges and convictions from His Word, and even gives us keen divine insight into our future, we must first submit to a wait.

Sacred Season

In Habakkuk 2:3, the Hebrew word for "appointed time" is *mow 'ed* which means "sacred season, set feast, appointed season and place." Let's focus our attention on the "sacred season" portion of the definition. These words help me think of God's timing for my life in a particularly stirring way.

In verse 3, the term *sacred* describes something set apart to bring God glory. Therefore, not only are events designed to bring Him glory but also the seasons in which those events occur. We mustn't attempt to rush God. To rush spoils the very reason God initially desired the event for us and cheats us of the joy that comes when we experience God's will. His plans are perfect without our input or interference.

How has God gotten glory from a painful season in your life?

_____

_____

Not long ago, Jerry planned a surprise date, but he made the mistake of letting me know about it without giving me any details. Being the impatient person I am, I kept interfering with his plans by asking questions and making suggestions.

The more answers I demanded, the more certain I became that Jerry was incapable of planning a big, fancy date without my help—at least that's how it seemed to Jerry. By the time the date night actually arrived, neither Jerry nor I felt excited by the event; the joy was gone.

I'd spent the whole week working so hard to make sure Jerry did everything "right" in planning our big surprise that I was exhausted. Worse, I had spoiled the evening. We would have both enjoyed the date so much more had I not been so anxious to have everything my way. Jerry's original plans were best without my suggested changes. My impatience and need for control ruined a beautiful evening.

God's "sacred seasons" for our lives can be like the date Jerry planned. God sometimes gives us pieces of information about what may occur but in our anxiousness to see it come to pass, we tweak the plans to fit our desires and goals. My root issue was my need to control the situation.

What practical things in your life do you try so hard to control you are wearing yourself out in the process?

_____

What does Ecclesiastes 3:11,14 say to you about the need to control?

_____

[I would have despaired] unless I had believed that I would see the goodness of the Lord in the land of the living. Wait for the Lord; Be strong and let your heart take courage; Yes, wait for the Lord.
Psalm 27:13-14, NASB

The passage reminds me not to so desperately try to control my future that I miss out on the beauty of today. I can relax in God's timing and enjoy God's gift of life.

In Psalm 27:13-14, David mentions the action he took to keep himself from losing heart as he waited on God to come through for him. He believed.

Believing is an action we must choose. A direct correlation exists between our level of belief and patience. Whether we believe God will do what He says will determine whether we can wait graciously for Him. Our lack of patience indicates we don't really believe the God we claim to trust.

In Genesis 15, God showed Abraham the heavens and told him that his descendants would be as numerous as the stars.

According to Genesis 15:6, what did Abraham do without receiving any

tangible proof that what God said was true?_____

How did the Lord respond to Abraham's action?

_____

What does this reveal to us about how God responds to those who take Him at His word?

_____

What part of the description of Abraham in Romans 4:20-21 impresses you most?

_____

What aspect of Abraham's faith would you most like to develop and why?

_____

_____

List the main thing(s) you are waiting for God to fulfill.

_____

What does your current patience level suggest about your belief in God's ability and character?

_____

Read Psalm 130:5 and Lamentations 3:25. Ask the Lord to help you, through the power of the Holy Spirit, to remain patient as you seek to wait on His timing in your life. Release control of your future to Him.

TAKE ACTION

As a summary of the study we've done together turn back through these pages. Particularly look at your answers. Write a letter. Address it to yourself, a loved one, to God, or even to me. Describe the lasting changes you desire for yourself as a result of the work you have done. And thank you for the chance to make this journey together.

_____

_____

_____

_____

_____

_____

Leader Guide

This leader guide provides directions for leading a seven-session group study. A leader kit is also available (001269687) containing DVDs with Priscilla's video messages to be used during the small-group sessions. While the video messages are valuable to the study, you may choose to do the study using only the member book. Each session in this guide suggests ways to use the DVDs and the material in the book.

Before each session arrange to have a DVD player in your meeting room. Complete each week's assignments. You do not have to have all the answers, but you need to be familiar with the material.

This leader guide is designed to be used for a 60-90 minute small-group session. In each session you will guide participants to understand and apply the concepts and principles they have studied during the week. More ideas have been provided than you will have time to use, so choose the activities that will best meet the needs of your participants.

If your group is too large for meaningful discussion to take place, consider breaking into smaller groups for discussion and coming together as a larger group to view the video.

Session 1

After this session participants will be able to—
• describe the purpose of the study;
• understand the format of the study.

Before the Session
1. Make a name tag for yourself. Provide pens and name tags for participants.
2. Preview video session 1.
3. Read the entire book to understand the purpose, content, and Bible-study method. Review the About the Session and Introduction sections and be ready to explain to participants what they can expect from the study. Examine the ideas

in the During the Session section that follows and decide which activities you will use.
4. Have copies of the member book available.

During the Session
1. As participants arrive, introduce yourself and direct them to the name tags and member books.
2. Welcome members. Explain that this session will overview the content, explain the learning approach, and allow members to get acquainted. Lead an opening prayer.
3. Overview the course. Explain that application is very important to this study. Say: *Your individual, daily study in the book will begin the process of application. However, the learning activities and discussion in each group session will continue that process. Together we will discuss concepts you studied during the week, and through several formats—reading, discussing Scripture, and watching video sessions—we will begin to flesh out the concepts and apply them to our lives.*
4. Direct members to complete the viewer guide on page 7 as they watch session 1. (Approx. 27 min.) If you choose not to use the video, present introductory information about the study.
5. Ask members to complete the lessons in week 1 of the member book before the next group session. Ask them to be ready to discuss the material.
6. Close with a prayer that participants will learn to hear God's voice.

Session 2

After this session participants will be able to—
• describe the sacrifices and rewards that come from walking obediently with God;
• identify ways to honor God;
• state steps to becoming dependent on God.

Before the Session

1. Provide markers and name tags. Be sure to wear your name tag as members arrive.
2. Study week 1 and complete the activities.
3. Preview video session 2.
4. Provide a chalkboard or dry erase board for use during the session.
5. Examine the following suggestions and decide which you will use during the session.

During the Session

1. Welcome everyone. Begin with prayer, asking God to bless participants during the session.
2. Ask, *According to Matthew 11:20, how did some adults respond to His miracles?* Follow up with a short discussion of how we respond today.
3. Say, *We read about sacrifices biblical characters made to walk obediently with God. What were the sacrifices and rewards of each mentioned in day 1:*
   • Peter and the apostles (Acts 5:17-29, 40-42)
   • Daniel, Shadrach, Meschach, and Abednego (Dan. 3:14-19, 27)
   • Abraham (Gen. 22:1-3, 16-18)
   • Joseph (Gen. 39:10-21; 41:41-42)
   • Hosea (Hosea 1:2-3; 3:1-3)
4. Ask, *According to Deuteronomy 28:1-14, what are the rewards promised to those who obey the Lord? Do we claim those promises today?*
5. Ask, *What is the difference between knowing Jesus and obeying Him?*
6. Ask several participants to define the phrase "the fear of the Lord is the beginning of wisdom."
7. Say, *On day 2 we learned that honoring God is key to hearing from God. How can we honor Him?* On a chalkboard write members' responses.
8. Share, *Humility is the ability to think of others, putting their needs before your own.* Ask members about people they know who are humble.
9. Ask several members to read the following verses aloud: Psalm 138:6; Isaiah 57:15; Isaiah 66:2; James 4:6; and James 4:10. After each verse is read, discuss what each teaches about humility.
10. Say, *Several times this week we looked at the different actions, behaviors, and responses we have*

during various life stages. Discuss some of these differences, especially as they relate to how we respond to God.
11. Have a member read Numbers 20:8-12. Discuss the story by following the questions on page 20.
12. Ask members to read Isaiah 7:9; John 3:18; John 8:24; and Hebrews 3:12. *Ask, According to these verses, what is the importance of faith in our relationship to the Lord?*
13. Read Psalm 131 and Matthew 18:1-4. From day 5, ask members to contrast statements from David and the disciples.
14. Ask, *What three steps must we take to become dependent on God? What is the difference between a calm and a quiet soul? What situations in our lives show times we need to depend on God?*
15. Direct members to the viewer guide on page 27. Show session 2. (Approx. 30 min.)
16. Conclude with prayer. Ask the Lord to give participants time and energy to study week 2.

Session 3

After this session participants will be able to—
• evaluate how they respond to God's glory;
• list three attributes of God;
• assess their motivations for "religious" activities.

Before the Session

1. Provide markers and name tags.
2. Study week 2 and complete the activities.
3. Preview video session 3.
4. Examine the following suggestions and decide which you will use during the session.

During the Session

1. Welcome everyone. Begin with prayer, asking God to bless participants during the session.
2. Read Exodus 3. Ask, *What can we learn about God's glory from Moses' encounter with Him?*
3. Assign members to read the following verses: Psalm 95:3; Jeremiah 10:16; Zechariah 4:14; 1 Thessalonians 1:9; Jude 25. Discuss how these verses illustrate God's incomparable power.

4. Ask, *How do we respond to God's glory? How did Moses and Isaiah respond?*

5. Ask, *From day 2, why did God tell Moses not to get closer and to remove his shoes?*

6. Read Romans 8:15 and Galatians 4:5. Ask, *How does our relationship with God compare to that of the Israelites?*

7. Ask, *What kinds of specific details did God give to the Israelites for the temple?*

8. Say, *Understanding God's attributes will help us grow to know Him in a deeper, more intimate way. In day 3 we examined three: power, mercy, and justice.* Break into three groups. One group will look at power; another, mercy; and another, justice. Have each group report their findings.

9. Say, *We are not made acceptable to God by who we are but by Whose we are. What is the only sacrifice ever needed for us to feel acceptable and adequate in God's sight?* Follow up by reading Hebrews 10:1-4.

10. Ask, *What is our position once we become Christians?* Have a member read Ephesians 2:6.

11. Ask, *According to Hebrews 7:22, what guarantees this covenant?*

12. Read Exodus 3:10-16 and 12:14-16. Ask several questions related to these passages:
    - What is Moses' main concern?
    - How did God redirect Moses' attention?
    - How can you relate to this scene?

13. Say, *We read in day 5 some of the things the Pharisees did to get noticed by other people.* Ask the following questions:
    - What are some of the "religious" things people do today to be noticed?
    - To gain acceptance?
    - Do these work?

    Say, *Christ was not impressed by the Pharisees. Would He be impressed by our shallow actions and behavior?*

14. Draw members' attention to the viewer guide on page 45 and ask them to fill in the blanks as you show video session 3. (Approx. 27 min.)

15. Conclude by asking participants if they have specific needs related to this study that they'd like the group to pray for. Divide into groups of two or three and pray together.

Session 4

After this session participants will be able to—
- identify three elements they receive with spiritual inheritance;
- relate to their lives the four reasons the children of Israel were to surrender to God;
- state why they should remember the promises God made—and kept—in the Old Testament.

Before the Session
1. Study week 3 and complete the activities.
2. Preview video session 4.
3. Secure a chalkboard or dry erase board.
4. Examine the following suggestions and decide which you will use during the session.

During the Session
1. Welcome everyone. Begin with prayer, asking God to bless participants during the session.
2. Ask, *Since your salvation, what signs do you see that your desires have changed?*
3. On the chalkboard, write *Worldly freedom* and *Freedom in Christ.* Ask the group to contrast the two.
4. Read Romans 6:12-13 to remind the group of God's challenge.
5. Ask two members to volunteer to write on the board. Have someone read Colossians 3:8,12-14. Ask the group to tell the volunteer writers what we must put on and take off as Christ's followers, according to these verses. Ask, *Which items would be most difficult to put on? take off?*
6. Ask members to state the three distinct elements we receive with our spiritual inheritance.
7. Read Joshua 24:14-15 from several Bible translations. Ask, *What ideas and concepts can you draw from reading the verse several times?*
8. Say, *In day 3 we learned Joshua gathered the people at Shechem. What is the significance of this place? Where is your "Shechem"?*

9. Ask, *What are the four reasons Joshua gave that the children of Israel should surrender to God, found in days 3 and 4? How do these relate to us today?*

10. Say, *In Genesis 12:2-3, God made a promise to Abraham. What was that promise?* Read Hebrews 11:12. Ask, *Did God keep that promise? What were some obstacles Abraham had to deal with?*

11. Ask, *What promises has God given you? What promises do you cling to?*

12. Say, *On day 4, we looked at the relationship between God and His chosen people.* Reread Joshua 24:4-12. Ask, *How has God protected you in order to preserve His calling and promises?*

13. Discuss the difference between obedience from the heart and ritual obedience. Close the discussion by reading Matthew 22:37.

14. Direct members to the viewer guide on page 65. Show video session 4. (Approx. 30 min.)

15. Before Priscilla closes the video session, you will see a music video. Use this as a prayerful, reflective time to be still before the Lord. This music video is also on disc 2 if you wish to use it in other sessions.

16. Conclude this group session by breaking into groups of three or four. Have each group share any prayer requests they have. Be sure the groups pray over these requests.

Session 5: A Still Attentiveness

After this session participants will be able to—
• identify the three questions they must consider for the battle in our minds;
• affirm Paul's six directives in Philippians 4:8 to fill our minds;
• assess how to alter their personal schedules to make time to sit before God.

Before the Session

1. Study week 4 and complete the activities.
2. Preview video session 5.
3. Examine the following suggestions and decide which you will use during the session.

During the Session

1. Welcome everyone. Open with prayer.
2. Ask, *What three questions must we consider for battle?*
   • Who is our enemy?
   • What are our weapons?
   • What is our battle strategy?
   Make sure members understand how these relate to the mental battle we fight.
3. Ask, *How is our faith like the Roman soldier's shield?*
4. Ask, *How can putting on the "helmet of salvation" cause you to walk more confidently?*
5. Ask, *What Scriptures can become daggers for you against Satan's attacks?* Use those in day 1 as examples to begin this dialogue.
6. Ask, *What six directives does Paul give in Philippians 4:8 to fill our minds?*
7. Read Ruth 1:5-22. Share, *Ruth put her trust in the God of her mother-in-law. Her faith didn't waver. She was obedient to God, regardless of her circumstances. In what circumstances does your faith waver? How have you been able to seek God in these times?*
8. Read 1 Timothy 1:15-16 and answer the questions from page 72.
9. Read Jesus' prescription to Levi in Luke 5:27. Ask, *How can you relate this to your life?*
10. Contrast Ruth's reaction to others:
    • Hannah—1 Samuel 1:6-7
    • Jonah—Jonah 4:1-3
    • King Ahab—1 Kings 21:4
11. Say, *In Exodus 14:13, we read that the Israelites were afraid as the Red Sea blocked their dreams of escaping slavery. Through Moses God said not to fear. Moses reminded the people God would fight for them.*
    Divide the large group into four groups. For each of the following, have the small group give the name of the person who needed encouragement and the situation: Genesis 15:1; Deuteronomy 31:6; 1 Chronicles 28:20; Isaiah 41:13. Ask each small group to share their answers with the large group.
12. Ask someone to read Ecclesiastes 2:11; Matthew 6:26-34; and John 14:27. Discuss how each speaks to the issue of our ambition.

13. Ask, *How might your ambition hurt your ability to hear from God?* Contrast with being still before God and letting Him control your ambitions.
14. Contrast the behavior of the Israelites found in Isaiah 30:1-2 and the resulting action from King Jehoshaphat's leadership in 2 Chronicles 20:6-12. Ask, *How did God respond to Jehoshaphat's prayer in 2 Chronicles 20:17?* Ask someone to rephrase this response in their own words.
15. Discuss how your schedule can be altered to make time to sit still before God.
16. Show video session 5. (Approx. 31 min.)
17. Conclude this group session with prayer, asking God to help you be still before Him.

Session 6

After this session participants will be able to—
• see the importance of divine interruption;
• explain the positive effects of God's Word on a Christian's life;
• state three indicators to determine if they are living outside God's will.

Before the Session
1. Study week 5 and complete the activities.
2. Preview video session 6.
3. Examine the following suggestions and decide which you will use during the session.

During the Session
1. Welcome everyone. Begin with prayer.
2. Ask members to tell of a time when God interrupted them, redirecting their plans to His.
3. Read Isaiah 55:8-9. Ask, *What do these verses reveal about the differences between our plans and the Lord's plans?*
4. Divide into three groups. Have each group review the case studies of Sarah, Claudia, and Tamara and report to the large group what can be learned about interruption from each.
5. Ask, *What two characteristics of the Bible do we learn in day two?* Follow up by asking, *What effect does the Bible have on our lives?*

6. Have several members read 2 Timothy 3:16-17 from different Bible translations.
7. Read John 14:21. Ask, *According to this verse, to whom will Christ reveal Himself?*
8. Ask someone to read Exodus 33:3-4. Lead discussion by asking the following questions:
   • How did the Israelites respond to Moses telling them God would withdraw from them?
   • How would you respond?
   • What was the reason God gave for possibly leaving them?
   • How do we normally respond to a stubborn and rebellious child?
   • How does God respond to us when we're stubborn and rebellious?
9. Ask, *What difference does having peace in your heart make in your life? your decisions?*
10. Contrast Jonah's and Jesus' reaction to being in the middle of a storm. Look at Jonah's example from Jonah 1:1-5. Read Jesus' reaction in Luke 8:23-24. Ask, *What did Jonah do? What about Jesus? Have you had sleepless nights because of a storm outside? What about a storm in your heart? How did you find peace?*
11. Ask, *What three indicators help us determine if we are living outside God's will?*
12. State, *We learned in day 5 that the Israelites expected victory as long as God's presence was evident. How do we respond today? What gives us the assurance that God is near even when we can't see Him physically?*
13. Ask volunteers to read: John 14:26; 16:8,13; and 2 Peter 1:3. Ask, *What can we do without the Spirit's help?*
14. Show video session 6. (Approx. 26 min.)
15. Conclude the session with prayer, asking God to help you to be hungry for His direction, His Word, His presence, His peace, and His power.

Session 7

After this session participants will be able to—
• recognize emotions they have during trials and willingly submit to God during these times;

- cite three elements of delighting in God;
- assess their willingness to wait on God's timing.

Before the Session

1. Study week 6 and complete the activities.
2. Preview video session 7.
3. Provide a chalkboard or dry erase board for use during the session.
4. If you'd like to celebrate finishing the study, plan to serve light refreshments. Ask several members to bring food, drinks, and utensils.
5. Examine the following suggestions and decide which you will use during the session.

During the Session

1. Welcome everyone. Begin with prayer, asking God to bless your session. Thank Him for the fellowship you've had these past weeks.
2. Have someone read 2 Timothy 1:8-9. Ask, *What do these verses mean in reference to being submissive to the Lord's assignment for us?*
3. Ask the group to read 1 Corinthians 12:4-11, allowing each person to read at least one verse. Write the gifts mentioned in these verses on a dry erase board or chalkboard. Follow up by saying, *We all have different gifts, just as we are all unique individuals. We can use these gifts to serve the Lord in what He has specifically for us to do.*
4. Say, *John 16:33 reminds us that we will have suffering and trouble in this world. What emotions do you typically have when you're facing trouble? How can you face trials with a Christ-like attitude?*
5. Break into three groups. Assign each group two biblical characters from the list in day 2. Have them summarize the challenges their characters faced and report their findings. After each group has reported, ask, *What can we learn from the experiences of these ordinary people?*
6. Ask for volunteers to read 2 Corinthians 4:17 and Philippians 3:20. Ask members to share a Scripture they noted on page 111 that helps them remember to keep an eternal perspective.
7. Read Psalm 37:4. Ask, *What are the three elements at the root of delighting in God?*

8. Ask the following questions regarding delighting in the Lord.
   - What things do we delight in?
   - How would someone recognize that we delight in that object, person, etc.?
   - What is the relationship between delighting in the Lord and our desires?
   - What is the relationship between delighting in the Lord and being content?
9. Have someone read 1 Samuel 3:1-10. Ask, *What does Samuel's response to Eli tell us about his general response to authority? Do we have a similar response?*
10. On a dry erase board or chalkboard, list authority figures in our lives. Solicit answers from the group. Discuss which might be easiest and most difficult to submit to and why.
11. Ask volunteers to give their summary of Romans 8:7.
12. Say, *Our study mentioned viewing submission as a gift for our good rather than a loss of freedom. What other picture describes the benefits of submission?* (If they need a reminder, direct them to page 116.
13. Say, *In day 5, we learned about being submissive to God's timing. What is the most difficult part of waiting? How willing are we to wait on God?*
14. Ask the group for reactions to the following statements from page 120: "Believing is an action we must choose. A direct correlation exists between our level of belief and patience. Whether we believe God will do what He said will determine whether we can wait graciously for Him."
15. Say, *This last video segment was filmed in Priscilla's home. In it, she reviews what we have learned during the past weeks.* (Approx. 16 min.)
16. Serve the refreshments if you've decided to include them in this session. Continue discussing what members have learned during the study.
17. Conclude with prayer, asking God to bless each participant as she seeks to position herself to hear God's voice.

Two Ways to Earn Credit
for Studying LifeWay Christian Resources Material

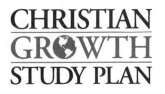

CHRISTIAN GROWTH STUDY PLAN

CONTACT INFORMATION:
Christian Growth Study Plan
One LifeWay Plaza, MSN 117
Nashville, TN 37234
CGSP info line 1-800-968-5519
www.lifeway.com/CGSP
To order resources 1-800-458-2772

Christian Growth Study Plan resources are available for course credit for personal growth and church leadership training.

Courses are designed as plans for personal spiritual growth and for training current and future church leaders. To receive credit, complete the book, material, or activity. Respond to the learning activities or attend group sessions, when applicable, and show your work to your pastor, staff member, or church leader. Then go to *www.lifeway.com/CGSP*, or call the toll-free number for instructions for receiving credit and your certificate of completion.

For information about studies in the Christian Growth Study Plan, refer to the current catalog online at the CGSP Web address. This program and certificate are free LifeWay services to you.

Need a CEU?

CONTACT INFORMATION:
CEU Coordinator
One LifeWay Plaza, MSN 150
Nashville, TN 37234
Info line 1-800-968-5519
www.lifeway.com/CEU

Receive Continuing Education Units (CEUs) when you complete group Bible studies by your favorite LifeWay authors.

Some studies are approved by the Association of Christian Schools International (ACSI) for CEU credits. Do you need to renew your Christian school teaching certificate? Gather a group of teachers or neighbors and complete one of the approved studies. Then go to *www.lifeway.com/CEU* to submit a request form or to find a list of ACSI-approved LifeWay studies and conferences. Book studies must be completed in a group setting. Online courses approved for ACSI credit are also noted on the course list. The administrative cost of each CEU certificate is only $10 per course.